PRIMED

YOUR GUIDE TO BUILDING AN **AMAZING BUSINESS** ON **AMAZON**

ADAM HUDSON

CONTENTS

FREE COURSE!

Want to build a thriving Amazon business? Get Adam's free Amazon course and learn:

- What the Amazon opportunity is
- How to find winning products that you can sell on Amazon
- The key financial levers that determine how much money you will make on Amazon
- The real truth about what it takes to be successful on Amazon

This industry leading course has educated thousands of people from more than 20 countries around the world.

Sign up today! It's totally free!

www.reliable.education/free-amazon-course

CHAPTER 1

★ ★ ★ ★ ★

THE **DISRUPTION** OF RETAIL

"Online retail is currently a $300B market in the US and growing to $1.5T by 2030."

> — *Marc Lore Founder of*
> *(sold to Walmart of $3B in 2015).*
> *Fortune TV interview 2015.*

Disruption, a term coined by Silicon Valley to describe what happens when technology fundamentally changes an entire industry, has undoubtedly arrived at the door of traditional retailing.

In the same way, Uber has facilitated enormous change within the personal transport business. AirBNB has become more valuable than any hotel chain on the planet within a 10-year period (without owning a single hotel). Amazon is the chief disruptor to the way people buy millions of everyday products, from diapers to TV sets, and almost everything in between.

To put in perspective how "landscape altering" the disruption of retail has been - in 2006, the largest publicly traded retailers in the US were Walmart, Target, Best Buy, Macys, Kohls, Nordstrom, JC Penny, and Sears. At that time, Amazon was worth less than 5% of their combined value.

In 2016, just ten years later, Amazon was worth more than all of them put together, and growing.

What's even more telling is the growth and decline of these companies as tabulated in the chart below.

COMPANY	MARKET VALUE 2006	MARKET VALUE 2016	%CHANGE
sears	$27.8B	$1.1B	↘ 96%
JCPenney	$18.1B	$2.6B	↘ 86%
NORDSTROM	$12.4B	$8.3B	↘ 33%
KOHL'S	$24.2B	$8.8B	↘ 64%
★macys	$24.2B	$11.0B	↘ 55%
BEST BUY	$28.2B	$13.2B	↘ 54%
TARGET	$51.3B	$40.6B	↘ 21%
Walmart	$214.0B	$212.4B	↘ 1%
amazon	$17.5B	$355.9B	↗ 1.934%

As you can see, of those eight American retailers from 2006 (who operate under the old "bricks and mortar" business model), all have <u>lost</u> value over the last ten years except Walmart. Walmart is only up 2% from its value a decade ago. By comparison, Amazon's value has grown by a stunning 1,910%.

These numbers define what "disruption" looks like. This is proof consumers have voted and they've chosen Amazon in a big way.

So what does this mean for you?

Well, if you have an entrepreneurial bone in your body, disruption is what you want to move towards.

Disruption means money is quickly moving from one place to another in large amounts. If you're early and smart, you can position yourself in line with this new money-route and participate in the transference of wealth, siphoning some of the money into your own pocket by adding value to those traveling along the new spending path.

I have been in business for more than 20 years, and never before have I seen such an incredible opportunity to build a global business that requires few, if any, employees. You can work from anywhere with an internet connection without investing a single cent into infrastructure or even marketing.

At the risk of sounding hyped-up and "gushy", what you're about to learn in this book may well be the finest business opportunity for the everyday person in the last 100 years. As cliché as that sounds, stick with me!

I'm about to teach you the basics of how to build a great business on Amazon, and I'll tell you about everyday people from all over the planet who, like me, are either making their full-time income on Amazon right now, or using Amazon to supplement their income for other purposes.

Most of these people are not hard-core entrepreneurs or people with rock-star personalities and sales skills. They are everyday people living in all kinds of places, from the beachside towns of Australia, to the jungles of Bali, to the cliffs of Maui, and the heartland of America.

So, why exactly am I so excited about the Amazon offer for those in search of more time, more money, and more, personal freedom?

Let's start with the first important thing about an Amazon business that surprisingly few small business owners ever really think about before jumping into a new business venture.

As an Amazon seller, you'll be selling products, not services.

Now this may sound simple, but it has taken me nearly twenty years to realize the importance of this fundamental choice about *how* you make money in business.

When I discovered the Amazon opportunity, I was living in Los Angeles California, running an animation company in Hollywood. We specialized in creating short animated videos explaining how things worked. Our clients ranged from large corporations, to startups, to small businesses of almost every kind.

Through a combination of excellent timing, unique service offering, and lots of hard work, I managed to build a thriving little studio boasting a list of clients that included Canon, MasterCard, World Bank, Volvo, Unicef, and Cox Communications. We were turning a nice profit, but something wasn't sitting well with me.

You see, the fundamental challenge with that kind of business is when someone makes an order. What they're really ordering is someone's <u>time</u>. In the case of the animation company, many people were involved, each of whom were responsible for different aspects of the project. There was the scriptwriter, the voice actor, the storyboard artist, the animator, and project manager. As the owner, my time was spent keeping all of these people paid and happy. It wasn't easy.

Compare a "time selling" business with a "product selling" business, and you'll quickly see a very different picture.

Over at my Amazon business I have no idea when a sale is even made. I get up in the morning and click on the Amazon app on my iPhone. Moments later, I am looking at how much money I've made whilst sleeping. It's what I call a "time-free" business, and it's extraordinary!

As I write this book, I sell about 10 products on Amazon in the US, Spain, Italy, Germany, France, the UK, Belgium, Luxembourg, Netherlands, Portugal, Ireland, Austria, Bulgaria, Cyprus, Czech Republic, Denmark, Estonia, Finland, Greece, Hungary, Latvia, Lithuania, Malta, Poland, Romania, Slovakia, Slovenia, and Sweden.

All of this and I have only one part-time employee in Thailand.

I have no office. I have no warehouses. I travel anywhere I want, whenever I want, and I do no advertising outside of a very small budget on Amazon's pay-per-click ads on Amazon itself. I don't run a website. I don't pack orders. I don't speak to a single customer. I simply get paid, every two weeks, from seven countries, in three currencies.

What's more, whilst brick and mortar competitors selling similar products wait for prospective customers to get into their cars, drive to their expensive shops to see one of their employees that earn an hourly wage (irrespective of whether or not there's anyone in that shop), I'm sitting back letting Amazon sell, pack, and ship my products (soon by drone) directly to my customers' homes. And because I save by <u>not</u> needing shops and redundant employees, I sell the same kinds of products for much less money.

Remember that I was talking about the best business opportunity of the last 100 years? What I am talking about here is a <u>totally</u> disruptive business model.

And here's the thing…

In my view, Amazon's dominance is only just beginning. While it's natural to assume a downturn is coming when your twenty-year growth history looks like the chart below, I believe that Amazon is the exception to the rule. I also believe it is due to its remarkable CEO, the founder of Amazon, Jeff Bezos.

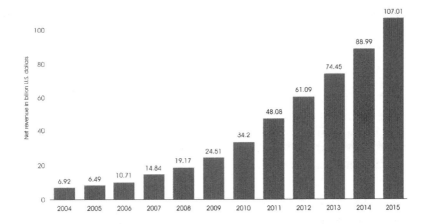

While most companies have buckled to the short-term desires of Wall Street, Amazon has declared almost no profits since it was founded over 20 years ago. Every year, Amazon has reinvested its profits and doubled down on its business model by raising capital through debt and other instruments to grow and invest in its future.

As a result, Amazon is light-years ahead of most of its competitors on a variety of technologies that will define the future of retail.

At the time of writing, they employ over 300,000 people and 40,000 robots. Amazon completed their first successful drone delivery to a real customer (in the UK) whereby the product was delivered to the customer within 13 minutes of them clicking the buy button!

Amazon has been such a prolific innovator, journalists around the world watch for new patent filings from the company. Many of these sound like tech-daydreams. For example, in a recent patent filing, it was revealed Amazon have come up with the idea of a blimp-like floating fulfillment center that would remain airborne above major cities around the world while drones fly in and out of "the mother-ship", removing the need for ground-based warehouses altogether, greatly decreasing cost and time of delivery from dollars to cents and days to minutes.

Believe it or not, these reasons are only part of why I believe Amazon is just getting started and why I believe there is a very good chance Amazon may be the world's first Trillion dollar company.

According to Amazon, their drones are already capable of delivering approximately 80% of the products they sell. If (or perhaps when) the US allows commercial drone deliveries (as UK has done), I believe we will see the next tectonic shift in retail, leaving the retail landscape looking unrecognizable from the prior decade.

Couple the arrival of widespread drone deliveries with Amazon's investments into Artificial Intelligence and hardware like Alexa, and there is a very good chance that within the next ten years you won't even visit a website like Amazon to order many consumable household items like food and toilet paper. Amazon will already know what you need and will simply ship it to you free if you're a Prime member.

Ok, so take a breath for a moment and bring this all back down to you, here and now. How can YOU make money from all of this?

Well, hopefully you get my point about selling products, not time. Now let me share something that totally blew my mind once I understood it.

Fulfillment By Amazon - or "FBA" as we sellers call it.

In the past, if you had your own line of products, you had only four choices for selling it:

1. You opened a retail store yourself.

2. You became a wholesaler and sold your product(s) to people or companies who owned retail stores.

3. You built a website and sold the product online, yourself.

4. You advertised the product on a third party retail website (like eBay) and then shipped the orders yourself, or paid a third party fulfillment service to do so for you.

These were your choices.

If, after what you've read in the preceding pages, option 1 still seems appealing, you should close this book and go buy a lottery ticket. Your chance of success is probably higher with the ticket.

Whilst option two (wholesaling) might sound appealing because you don't have to face the consumer or lease shops, there's still a number of issues to consider. Who will warehouse your products? Who will ship them to your retailers? How long will it take the retailers to pay you? Can you afford to supply all of your retail client's stores credit for 60 or 90 days? Can you make a high enough profit margin if you're selling at wholesale prices instead of full retail prices?

In recent times, many people have opted for options three and four above, which (setting Amazon aside) are, in my opinion, far better ways to go. This being said, neither get you there if lifestyle is your goal.

If I had a dollar for every amazing website someone built that didn't make money, I'm sure I'd be a very rich man. You see, having a great product and a beautiful website means nothing if you don't have people visiting the site. Attracting people to websites is a very expensive business and requires specialized knowledge that either you or someone you hire has to have.

When you sell on Amazon, there are millions of customers going to their websites every day. All you have to do is be there!

The last option, selling on a marketplace like eBay (for example), was my favorite idea prior to Amazon because it solved the massive issue of an everyday person having to build a website and drive traffic to it, but it still required that someone ship the product. "No big deal", you might think, "I don't mind doing that". But what about if you want to go to Europe for a family vacation? Who will take care of the business then?

Enter Fulfillment By Amazon (FBA), a game changing model enabling anyone to attract global sales and world-class distribution from day one without any employees or capital investment

Here's how it works.

If you want to sell on Amazon in the UK (for example), you need three things:

1. Amazon seller account in the UK (about $40/month).

2. Inventory in one of Amazon's UK fulfillment centers (my inventory is in London).

3. A sales page on amazon.co.uk (takes about 1 hour to setup).

That's it.

You don't need to go there. You don't need to know anyone there. You don't need to hire anyone there. You don't need to build a website. You don't need to arrange a shopping cart for the website or arrange credit card processing facilities. You don't need to learn Facebook marketing or Google AdWords.

The same applies if you want to sell on Amazon in America.

No matter where you live, you can sell into countries all over the world with Amazon, following just these three steps.

Japan? Hai! (Japanese for YES). Italy? Si! Germany? Ja! You can start wherever you want, with as little or as much as you have, and you're in.

Compare this to the old model of trying to get your products into Walmart's brick and mortar stores. Legend has it that it takes months just to get a meeting. If you get a meeting, you have to convince them. If they like your product, they'll negotiate so hard you'll barely make any money. If you agree, they'll want enough inventory to stock a bunch of their stores which, most likely, you can't afford to supply at the necessary quantity, much less on the payments terms they'll want.

It is basically a lockout for small retailers trying to get into the game.

Amazon, on the other hand, <u>want</u> their customers to have as many choices as possible, so they have a business model that enables getting into Amazon easy and super affordable!

Amazon requires minimal initial commitment and they charge only $40/month for professional selling privileges. From there, you only pay fees on what you sell (which I'll get into soon).

Today, I have inventory in just two Amazon warehouses (London and Dallas), and my products are sold into more than 30 countries from these two locations. I have not been to either warehouse, ever. Remarkable!

The end result of using Amazon's FBA service is simple:

- Amazon runs the website.
- The website already has customers going to it so I spend almost nothing on advertising.
- When a sale is made, Amazon pick, pack and ship the order from a warehouse they pay for, staff, and insure.
- Amazon handles all returns and exchanges.
- Amazon handles 90% of my customer service.

I literally spend less than 20 minutes a day working on my Amazon business, and it's a seven figure a year business.

This model is a stroke of genius on Amazon's part. Their customers get an unparalleled level of choice and service. Amazon gets to control the customer experience but they charge sellers, such as me, to use it. Everybody wins!

What's really exciting is once you've developed your brand and line of products (as I'll teach you in this book), you can keep growing simply by putting the same line of products on Amazon markets and in their warehouses all over the world.

At the time of writing this book, Amazon was planning to open fulfillment centers in Australia and Singapore. All it would take for any Amazon seller in the world to access customers in those markets via Amazon would be the same three steps:

1. Open an Amazon seller account in the country.

2. Put inventory into the local fulfillment center.

3. Create a sales page on the local Amazon website.

No trips "down under" or into Asia are required if you want to sell to Australians or Singaporeans! Just call your supplier and get a shipment into Amazon's warehouse there and you're in business and earning Aussie dollars and Singapore dollars on top of your USD, Pounds, and Euros!

Ka-Ching!

Hopefully by now you're starting to see why I am so enthusiastic about what Amazon offers the everyday person when it comes to building a time-free, location-free income, right from wherever they are, without many of the roadblocks, risks, and expenses of the old, traditional method of selling products online.

If you're willing to learn something new, and to open your mind to something truly outside of the box, then let's get stuck in and learn how to create an incredible global business, working hand-in-hand with one of the most successful companies in history, Amazon!

CHAPTER 2

★★★★★

VELOCITY RETAILING

"Compound interest is the most powerful force in the universe"

— *Albert Einstein*

Sadly, when it comes to business opportunities of almost every kind, there are always those telling you everything is easier, faster and less expensive than it really is. Amazon is no different.

A quick Google search of "learn to make money on Amazon" will turn up thousands of results with headlines like "Amazon Secrets Revealed", "Your path to easy riches on Amazon", "Amazon Cash Machine" etc.

This is a real shame because most of these courses set people up for failure by raising their expectations to unrealistic levels, ruining what is otherwise a remarkable opportunity to build a reliable, long-term business on Amazon.

In the interests of full-disclosure, I *do* sell an Amazon course as well. It is, however, very different to almost all courses I've ever seen on the subject, and I've seen a lot of them.

My course is called "Reliable Income". Notice how it's not called "Quick Income", "Easy Income" or "Massive Income"? That's because my research revealed most people don't actually want these things. What they want is a <u>reliable</u> income allowing them the freedom to spend more time with their families and less time stuck in a job they don't necessarily love.

Once learned, these fundamentals are not difficult to master and there's no real magic to them. Mostly it's logic and your ability to delay your gratification until such time as your base is strong enough to support the income you want from your Amazon business.

Before I begin, I want to share with you a fascinating study done in 1970 that put a group of 5-year-old kids into an observation room where each was presented with one marshmallow on a plate. The children were told that they could either eat the marshmallow now, or they could wait 20 minutes and they would receive a whole bag of marshmallows. Of those tested, only a few waited the 20 minutes.

The researchers then tracked those children for the next 40 years, studying their professional and financial progress. Using no other metric other than their ability to wait 20 minutes for a bag of marshmallows when they were 5 years old, those that had waited the 20 minutes became far more successful financially.

Fascinating!

For most everyday people who will be starting an Amazon business with modest financial means but a desire for time-free income, the same principle of delayed gratification will need to apply.

Why?

Because you make money on Amazon in only one way - selling products. The more products you have, the more money making potential you have. The fewer products you have, the less money making potential you have.

In simple terms, your income is directly tied to how much inventory you have, and how much inventory you have will be tied to how much capital you have.

Sadly, very few Amazon gurus make this point clearly. Instead, they keep you focused on how much money you can make with little mention of the underlying investment in inventory that is required.

Much like the game of monopoly, each product you have on Amazon is like a house. The more houses you have, the more income you make. Every now and then, you'll launch a product that becomes a hotel. These are hit products people love and they are visited more often than your houses. These "hotel products" earn way more than your average "house product" on the Amazon monopoly board.

Make sense?

That being said, houses and hotels cost money to buy, so if you have limited cash to start with, then you're going to have to be patient, follow Jeff Bezos' strategy, and reinvest what you earn into your business. Over time, you'll build a nice little portfolio of houses and hotels and you'll be able to retire from your Amazon income.

So here's my "Velocity Retailing" formula to help get your head around this. Before I explain it though, I want you to understand that the examples used are only to demonstrate the power of compounding your profits (rather than spending them) to grow the value of your underlying asset (your inventory). These calculations do not account for taxation on your profits as you make them. Taxation will impact these numbers and vary greatly from country to country.

Capital x Return x Rotations = Income

Ok, let's begin with the second variable, "Return".

I have a saying that goes like this.

"In business, turnover is irrelevant. It's the <u>left over</u> I'm interested in."

For some strange reason, many experts are always talking about how much "revenue" they're doing on Amazon, but revenue numbers can be very misleading. What's the point of doing $1,000,000 in revenue if your costs are $1,000,001?

It's somewhat important to know that second part right?

When I say, "return", I am referring to the percentage return you make on the capital you invested. For example, if you invest $1 into a product that sells on Amazon and you get $1.30 back after paying for all the costs, then your *return* is 30%.

Income	$1.30
Capital invested	$1.00
Profit	$0.30

$0.30 is 30% of $1 so your return is 30%.

The next piece of the formula is "Rotations". Rotations relates to how many times a year you can sell that inventory and realize that return. For example, if you order 1,000 frying pans for $10,000, how quickly will you be able to get your money back and order them again? Can you rotate 1,000 frying pans once, twice or even three times a year?

As you'll see in a moment, the answer to this question will have a profound impact on the amount of money you'll make as an Amazon seller.

The last piece is "Income". This is simply how much money you'll actually make from your Amazon business - after ALL expenses.

So let me give you a practical example, and then we will dive deeper into some of the variables and how they can greatly impact your spendable income.

Jake is a stay-at-home dad raising three beautiful kids, while his wife Sally continues to run the graphic design business they started 5 years before having a family. They both have an eye for design and they spot a gap in the market for high-end kids' dinner plates. In total, they want to invest $10,000 into starting an Amazon business.

They've done their research and found a supplier in China who will put their own designs onto the plates they want, at a price of $5 for a set of four plates.

In addition to the cost of the plates, they will spend a further $3/set on beautiful packaging to really make their product stand out. On top of that, Jake and Sally will be paying $1.30 per set to ship them to the US, and an additional $0.70c/set for import duties. So here's what that looks like:

Plates	$5.00
Packaging	$3.00
Freight	$1.30
Duties	$0.70
Total	$10.00/set

For the purposes of this book, we will refer to this $10 total as "The Cost Of Goods Sold", or "COGS" for short. It represents the total cost of getting your *complete* product made and then shipped all the way to Amazon's warehouse and ready for sale.

Please note these costs are for demonstration purposes only. Different types of products attract different import duties depending on what they are and where they are from. Obviously, freight charges vary widely as well, depending on the size and weight, and where the products come from. For now, though, all I want you to understand is the concept of COGS.

So now, Jake and Sally are faced with setting a retail price for their plates on Amazon. When they look at the top listings for similar items, they learn that their competitors are selling four plain white kids' dinner plates for around $16.99, but theirs have stunning designs and they are packaged and photographed to a much higher standard. They strongly feel that because of these additional touches, they can get $21.99/set.

So, how much money will they actually make per set of plates they sell?

To figure this out, we need to know the additional costs of selling the plates on Amazon. Here follows a breakdown of what Amazon charges on most items.

There are four main fees:

- Order handling fee
- Pick & Pack fee
- Weight handling fee
- Referral fee (Amazon's commission - 15% on most items)

Using Amazon's free online fee calculator (Google "Amazon FBA Fee Calculator" to find it as the URL changes from time to time), they discover they will be paying the following fees on each sale.

Order handling fee	$1
Pick & pack fee	$1.06
Weight handling fee	$2.30
Referral fee	$3.29 (Amazon's sales commission)
Total selling costs	$7.65/unit

OK, take a breath; we are almost done with the math!

In short, Amazon will be taking $21.99 from the customer. They will retain $7.65/unit for their fees, and they will add the difference to Jake and Sally's seller account that is distributed to them every two weeks by direct bank transfer.

Here's how that looks:

Customer pays	$21.99
Amazon keeps	-$7.65
Jake and Sally get	$14.34/sale

So how much are Jake and Sally actually making?

Well, they get $14.34 in income from Amazon and then they have to deduct their COGS ($10).

So on every sale, after paying Amazon's fees and after paying for their product, packaging, freight and duties (COGS), it looks like this:

Customer pays	$21.99
Amazon keeps	-$7.65
Jake and Sally get	$14.34/sale
Less COGS	-$10.00/unit
Actual profit	$4.34/unit

OK, now that might not look too exciting at first pass, but stick with me!

To make $4.34, they actually only invested $10 for the unit. $4.34 is 43.4% of the $10 that they risked. To work this out, simply get a calculator and put in 4.34 divided by 10.

In short, they earned a 43% return on their money in the time that it took to get the product made and then sold on Amazon.

With their $10,000 in startup capital, they can buy 1,000 units at $10/set. So every time they sell those 1,000 sets they earn:

1,000 x $4.34 = $4,340

This is what we call a "Rotation". Remember the formula?

Capital x Return x <u>Rotations</u> = Income

If it takes them 6 months to "rotate" those plates, it means they can earn that $4,340 twice a year, all from that same $10,000 in capital.

Make sense?

So here's where it gets really exciting.

$4,340 x 2 rotations = $8,680/year income.

$8,680/year income from $10,000 invested? That's a whopping 86.8% return on their money annually!

Ok - time to hit the pause button because this is truly extraordinary!

While most people might think, "Well that's great, but I can't live on $8,680/year", let me highlight something. Warren Buffet, the world's #1 investor, has averaged about 20% annual return throughout his career. Is it possible that Jake and Sally and their humble dinner plates have just outperformed the world's best investor?

Many people have spent $100,000 or more to setup a traditional small business or franchise, only to find themselves tied into leases, selling their time, watching their lives tick by locked inside a room all day.

What if Jake and Sally invested $100,000 and started earning 86.8% annually on that money? That would be $86,800/year and they could be anywhere in the world to earn that income, without needing a lease, an office or any employees!

I know you can go to Google and find a million stories of people who are apparently making far more money on Amazon than I am showing you here. And, apparently, with far less capital invested. But now you know the math and how it works, you can easily see the trick they *don't* reveal, which is income only comes AFTER you've invested money into inventory.

So this begs the question: "If I only have $10,000 to start with, and that's only going to make me $8,680/year, how do I get enough inventory to earn my goal of making, say, $80,000 per year on Amazon? Does it mean I need 10 times that $10,000 investment?"

Well, this would certainly be one way to get there, but I want to teach you a couple of other things before we explore that question.

The point of me teaching you my Velocity Retailing Formula is so that you understand the levers to determine how much money you'll actually have to spend or reinvest back into your business.

Remember the marshmallow test? Jake and Sally could spend that $8,680/year if they wanted, but because they're smart, and they understand the power of compound growth, they decide that they will reinvest the $8,680 each year into more inventory. Over time (and not a lot of time), things get really interesting.

Here's what happens to $10,000 that is compounded at a rate of 86%/year:

End of year 1	$18,680
End of year 2	$34,744
End of year 3	$64,624
End of year 4	$120,200
End of year 5	$223,572

Whaaaat?!

$10,000 becomes $223,572 after five years?

So Jake and Sally could have started *spending* their $8,680/year back in year one (like the kids who couldn't wait for the bag of marshmallows), or they could reinvest their profits each year and delay their gratification, building a strong inventory base that will produce *much* more income in the future.

Now let's look at the position they're in 5 years later.

First, their $10,000 investment has turned into an asset (inventory) worth $223,572. That's a staggering 2,223% growth.

But what's important from a lifestyle point-of-view, is that they now have $223,572 invested into an environment that is producing an 86% return annually. Assuming they simply sell that inventory twice a year and spend all the profit on themselves (no more investing for growth), that's $192,271/year in income. Not bad from a $10,000 investment five years earlier.

If you think that's amazing, let me show you the best part. There is a very good chance that Jake and Sally are now very close to becoming millionaires and they don't even know it!

You see, what Jake and Sally have really built here is a business. A good business plenty of people would like to buy. Who wouldn't want to walk into an already built business producing $192,000/year profit while the owners don't have to be any-where in particular, tied to a lease, or have a single employee?

In my opinion, Jake and Sally could easily get 3 times their annual profit plus the value of their inventory if they decided to sell.

Here's how that might look:

3 x $192,271 =	$576,815
Inventory value =	$223,572
Sale price	$802,387

If they decide to invest their profit for one more year at 86%, they're definitely going to reach millionaire status, all from $10,000, some hard work, and a good dose of patience.

Can you see why I get frustrated with gurus who feel they have to hype people up and mislead them through the omis-sion of basic math? This is an astounding opportunity without any of that!

Now it's time to cool our heels a little and talk about the reality of this journey. Plain and simple, businesses don't go in straight lines. First, not all products will earn a 43% return (mine average 39%) but the average across Amazon is probably much lower.

In this book, I will teach you how to go for premium prices and not compete in low margin niches. That having been said, the return in the Jake and Sally example is just shown for the sake of demonstrating the math principles.

Second, sometimes products don't fire. If you follow the advice in this book, your chance of that happening will be considerably lower. However, in the event you miss the market, you may have to sell out your product and recover your COGS. Unless you've done something really wrong, this shouldn't be hard to do because you're basically going to be selling your items at wholesale prices to recover your capital.

Finally, what *wasn't* shown in the example above is the cost to establish a brand and a new product on Amazon. If you are going to create a line of well-packaged and well-branded kids' dinner plates like the Jake and Sally example, you'll need a logo, a package design, and awesome photography.

I'll get into details around these later in the book, but these three things could cost $2,000 to have done professionally. This is a one-time investment into your brand and listing, but something to keep in the back of your mind.

As you'll learn, I don't believe in doing the absolute minimum to start a business. That's what most people do and it's the most dangerous place to start, in my opinion.

The truth is there are all kinds of variables and things unfore-seen that may happen in business. That's why so few people choose this path.

Before I finish this chapter, I want to explain *why* I have the Velocity Retail Formula at all. Sure, it's a great way to work out what you will actually make from your Amazon business, but there's another reason as well.

Each of these variables, Capital, Return, and Rotations, may have a massive impact on your income.

For example, if you have the same capital but tweak the return and/or the rotation frequency even a little, you will increase or decrease your income <u>dramatically</u>.

For example, in the Jake and Sally story, their numbers were:

$10,000 Capital x 43.8% Return ($4,340) x 2 Rotations = $8,680/year income

What if, instead of selling heavy, relatively bulky dinner plate sets, they were selling a small and light item that their supplier kept on hand instead of them having to wait for their product to be manufactured each time? Something like golf balls or gardening gloves? This would mean that they wouldn't have to account for manufacturing time or allow a full month just for the boat to go from China to the US because they could airfreight the goods and have them in three days.

By tweaking the number of *rotations* each year, they would see a dramatic impact on their income, without their 43% *return* or their *capital* base changing.

So let's see what happens if they can rotate their $10,000 just one extra time a year, three times instead of twice a year. How does this play out?

$10,000 Capital x 43.8% ($4,340) x 3 rotations = $13,020/year income

The return on their $10,000 goes from 86.8% annually to 130.2% annually.

If you run those numbers out over the same 5 years of compounding, here's how it looks. I'll use 130% to make it simpler:

End of year 1	$23,000
End of year 2	$52,900
End of year 3	$121,670
End of year 4	$279,841
End of year 5	$643,634

The *same* capital, compounded at the *same* rate of return, for the *same* five-year period, but *rotated* just one extra time a year, and instead of having an inventory base of $223,572 at the end, you have an inventory base of $643,634.

One extra rotation and you're up almost 300%.

Even more astounding, if you stop reinvesting at that point, and start spending the 130% return on your higher inventory base, you're now earning 130% on $643,634.

That's a staggering $836,724 a year.

Sell that business for 3 x earnings + the inventory and it looks like this:

3 x $836,724 =	$2,510,172
Inventory value =	$643,634
Sale price	$3,153,806

All from $10,000 invested five years earlier. Who knew *not* eating marshmallows right away could be so profitable?

So my point is *not* that this is normal, easy, or will happen. My point is simply that you understand the impact of what seem like small things compounded over time.

Remember the quote at the start of this chapter?

"Compound interest is the most powerful force in the universe"

— *Albert Einstein*

Albert was a pretty bright guy and he wasn't kidding!

I encourage you to sit down and use my Velocity Retailing Formula to map out *your* financial goals and see what *you* need to make happen in order to live the life that *you* want. If you have a partner, sit down with them as well.

If you're one of those people who hate numbers and you skipped over this work, then let me be the first to tell you, <u>this</u>

<u>isn't good enough!</u> Business *is* numbers. If you don't know ~~your~~ numbers then you are not in business.

This kind of deep understanding of fundamentals is what many small business people lack and why so few ever succeed. One of my mentors and favorite authors is Robert Kiyosaki. Robert's "Rich Dad" series of books educate millions of people on financial literacy, literacy that will change your financial life.

Here are three books I strongly recommend you read:

1. Rich Dad Poor Dad - By Robert Kiyosaki
2. The Richest Man In Babylon - By George S. Clason
3. The Dip - By Seth Godin

These books contain incredibly powerful teachings around money and what it takes to succeed in life and business.

Here's a few questions that often come up when I explain the Velocity Retailing Formula and use the Jake and Sally story as an example:

When they get their capital back, together with their return, do they keep buying more of the same dinner plates? Surely, they wouldn't have $200,000 worth of the same dinner plate in stock in five years' time!

That's a great point and you're right. They probably wouldn't keep reinvesting into the same item. Instead, once they have enough dinner plates to stay in stock year-round, they will probably launch a second product. It may be another design or they might launch cups or some other kids' eating accessories.

What you must remember, is if you only have $10,000 to start with, you probably will need more stock than you can afford just to keep up with the demand for the item on Amazon, and that's just in the US.

Rather than designing and launching a second product, Jake and Sally may decide to use their profits to launch the same dinner plate set in the UK market. This is really smart because it would require almost no new work.

In short, there are several ways they might deploy their profits to grow. It depends on their niche, personal desires, and their specific goals.

Warren Buffet is an investor but this is a business. How did you make that comparison?

Here's the thing about having an Amazon business. If you use Fulfillment By Amazon (where they handle the entire ware-housing, shipping etc.), then once you set it up, it acts far more like an investment than it does a business. I spend between 1-2 hours a week on my Amazon business, whereas even a passive investor probably reads for this amount of time, to stay abreast of what's happening in the markets. They, too, have a lot of risk, so I personally feel you *can* compare owning an Amazon business to managing an investment portfolio.

Is a 43% return high for Amazon?

Amazon has always been the place to go for low prices and this continues to be the case, especially as more and more people are competing for the sale. Irrespective, in this book I will show you my counter-intuitive (yet, very logical) strategy of moving toward premium products and staying away from products where price is the main driver.

Putting things in perspective though, even if you made only 20% return and rotated twice year, that's a 40% annualized return. These kinds of returns put you way ahead of almost any other strategy for growing your wealth over time.

I'm excited! I have $100,000 right now. Should I go "all in", or should I do this gradually?

My advice is always to go slowly. Money is very hard to make and very easy to lose. So let's look at the real cost of testing the waters first.

Instead of investing the whole $100,000 now, why don't you start with $10,000 to see if you can get it back, plus your return (let's say 30%). If this takes six months, then the worst case scenario is you now know how it works and you've proven to yourself you can do it.

Now go up to $50,000 wait another six months, and repeat the process.

If you do this twice, you really minimize your risk and you'll feel better about making a bigger investment on your next order. In total, you may lose a year by going in slowly, but how long did it take you to get that $100,000 after tax? For most people this is a lot of money, so be careful until you know what you're doing!

My advice with Amazon is always this.

Be patient!

This is not the kind of business you rush. Undertaking research, dealing with suppliers, getting samples, waiting for boats - all of this takes *time*.

In the Jake and Sally story, Amazon gets $7.65 for every sale. That's 34% of the retail price. This seems really high, doesn't it?

Businesses cost money, plain and simple. For this $7.65, which you *didn't* have to risk upfront, you received an incredible amount of value.

Here's some of it:

- You got to use Amazon's brand. That carries massive trust and value.
- You got to use their multi-billion dollar logistics infrastructure.
- You got to use their warehouse receiving staff to unload your truck and check your items into inventory.
- You got to use their staff to pick, pack, and send your order when a sale was made.
- You didn't have to build the website.
- You didn't have to do any advertising.
- You didn't have to learn how to use Facebook or Google.
- You don't have to handle returns.

- You didn't have to go to the post office.
- You didn't have to hire anyone.
- You didn't have to provide insurance to cover warehouse employees.
- You didn't have to train staff.

The list goes on.

Basically, Amazon lets you lease their whole infrastructure and all their people on a no-contract, performance-only basis - anywhere in the world where they do business. It's an absolutely innovative offer.

Can I spend less on logos, packaging and photography?

Yes! There are millions of products on Amazon and it does not make sense to have premium design work done for all of them. In the next chapter, "What Kind Of Animal Are You?" I explain the different types of Amazon business models and how each one differs in strategy.

What is important is that, unlike most Amazon sellers, you are prepared to invest money where it matters. Too many people go into business attempting to invest as little as possible because they think it's reducing their risk. In my view, this thinking is profoundly flawed because it presupposes your customers won't notice that you skimped on quality. This fundamental error in judgment may prove very expensive.

In my experience, people are sick of low quality, cheap products that may have been misrepresented to the market. I think the riskiest thing you can do is assume your customer is stupid.

CHAPTER 3

★ ★ ★ ★ ★

WHAT KIND OF **ANIMAL** ARE YOU?

Amazon is a large and thriving jungle, offering all kinds of ways to make money. Much like a real jungle, there are microclimates that enable some life forms to thrive while others struggle to survive, and there are seasons that give certain products life cycles for just a few months at a time.

With many different products and a vast landscape, it is important to know what kind of animal you are, and which corner of the jungle you should head towards in order to thrive.

For the purposes of this chapter, I am going to divide the wildlife into just 3 different animals:

- Lions
- Monkeys
- Peacocks

What it takes to be a successful Lion is different from what it takes to be a successful Monkey or a successful Peacock. They are vastly different animals that think, act and survive in very different ways.

As you've seen from previous chapters, Amazon is a thriving marketplace, and as such, more and more animals are moving in everyday. Each different product niche is a unique microclimate with its own set of rules and conditions, and within each microclimate, at least two of these three animals are competing, but thankfully not always for the same meal.

Let me give you an example:

If you look at the pills and potions microclimate, an area of the jungle where travelers go to find everything from Vitamin C tablets to protein powders to weight loss supplements and sleep aids, this area of the jungle is thriving. There are millions of travelers, and tens of thousands of animals trying to sell their wares.

In the past, this microclimate was dominated by Lions; big, multi-national brands, turning out all kinds of pills and potions. It was easy hunting. The margins were incredible. The products are often sourced domestically (meaning fast shipping times and no import duties), and the products usually small and un-breakable. In addition to all this, pills and potions are the kinds of products that travelers come back and buy over and over because they are consumable. Most of all, millions of travelers arrived at this microclimate everyday. The Lions lived well.

On Amazon, though, Monkeys now rule this microclimate. Monkeys are nimble, highly active, very smart marketers who made their own lines of pills and potions and spend all day swooping on customers before Lions get there.

These Monkeys are extremely good sales people and quickly guide buying travelers to their well-packaged and well-marketed products before Lions even see them. Lions are having trouble keeping up!

Sometimes these Monkeys even work in teams, alerting each other to new opportunities and working together to take as much business from Lions and other Monkeys as possible.

If you love marketing and want to spend your days watching the jungle for any sign of movement and change, then maybe you're a Monkey. Successful Monkeys do very well on Amazon, often making hundreds of thousands of dollars a month in sales, but it's a game where only the fittest survive.

If the product is:

- Easily sourced
- Highly sought after by lots of travelers
- Has high margin
- Is not necessarily dependent on a brand name
- Is in-demand year round
- Consumable (purchased over and over)

Know that Monkeys will abound! You have to be very smart, very active, and willing to invest in marketing and other promotions every single month to survive.

Now let's look at another microclimate. Toothpaste. Although Toothpaste could be classed as a potion, it's a very different kind of potion, to say, an anti-aging eye serum.

To demonstrate this point, name two specific brands of anti-aging eye serum for me. Hmmm. Not sure, right?

Now name two specific brands of toothpaste. If you're like most people, you have no idea who makes eye serum, but you easily name Crest, Colgate, or perhaps Sensodyne. Why is that?

The Lions have spent Billions of dollars making sure you believe that when it comes to toothpaste, a product almost every person in America uses at least once a day, you know these three products are the ones you can trust to put into your mouth.

I am sure the Monkeys have probably tried to break into the Toothpaste microclimate, but if you go to Amazon and look up "Toothpaste", you find that Lions dominate the first page, and they ain't going to give up this turf easily. It is sacred ground because literally every American uses this product throughout their entire life, once or twice a day.

Sure, Monkeys could get together and give it a go, but Lions have very deep pockets and they'll simply drop their prices and sell their product below cost if they have to, until they choke out the Monkeys who cannot survive nearly as long without the oxygen of a profit margin. Even the richest Monkeys are poor in comparison to the Lions in this microclimate.

So, what about these Peacocks? Who are they, where do they thrive, and why?

Peacocks are nowhere near as active or as smart as the Monkeys, but when it comes to beauty, they have no equal. In fact, some Peacocks are so famous for their remarkable colors and feather displays, travelers come from far and wide just to say they've seen one.

Unlike Monkeys who constantly jump from branch-to-branch studying the jungle minute-by-minute, Peacocks don't chase travelers or move much at all. Instead, discerning travelers seek them out and even the most persistent Monkey does not easily sway them.

Want to see some Peacocks? OK, let's jump over to the microclimate where Men's Watches are sold.

Now, before I explain the subtle nuances of this microclimate, let me point out there are some Peacocks so rare, so beautiful, and so famous in this area of the jungle, they literally don't have to compete at all. In fact, travelers simply type in their name and will look at nothing else.

Not only that, but these discerning travelers will pay as much as 10,000 times the price of any other Peacock, or Monkey's, product, even though it will do the same thing, just because it is sold by a particular Peacock.

How wonderful would it be to be one of those rare birds?

By now you've probably caught on I am talking about the difference between buying a $50 no-name watch, and a $50,000 Rolex. Yes, you can buy Rolexes on Amazon for this amount and much more!

Wait a minute Adam, are you saying I should set my sights on competing with the Rolex's of the jungle? Well no, I don't think you should try to compete directly with them, but yes, if you're not a Monkey at heart, then I think you should learn from the Rolex's of the jungle and apply those lessons to your own brand on Amazon.

In fact, let me tell you about a young man who did exactly this, who, as I write this book, is making around $4,000,000 a week in sales being a Peacock in the Men's Watch microclimate. His name is Filip Tysander, and he's from Sweden.

In 2006, Filip was backpacking through Australia when he met a fellow traveler named Daniel. Daniel was an elegant guy who possessed a sense of style which caught Filip's attention. He was rugged and understated, but what got Filip's attention was Daniel's watch. It had a minimalist black and grey nylon band, but the timepiece itself was a Rolex Submariner - a $7,000 timepiece.

Although the Submariner is an expensive watch, in it's simplest form (without a solid gold band for example), it's quite an understated timepiece. This combination of rugged practicality and understated luxury got Filip thinking.

"What if I create a line of watches that juxtaposed these two things, and what if I sell them at a fraction of the cost of a Rolex but brand it in such a way that it looks and feels equally special?"

Filip got to work.

Starting with just $15,000 in 2009, Filip's company grew very quickly. In 2014, following his simple brand idea, Filip sold more than a million watches and took in more than $70,000,000 in revenue. In a 2015 interview with Bloomberg, Filip was estimating sales of $220,000,000 for that year. Who knows where he is today.

In case you're interested, Filip called the company after his travel buddy, Daniel Wellington, and today his watches are sold all over the world.

Like all great Peacocks, Filip created a brand and range of products possessing a unique sense of style appealing to a very specific type of jungle traveler. His watches are sourced from China, but they *look* as if a leading European watchmaker designs them. They retail for between $150 and $300, making them affordable to his target market, while still well above the many super-cheap watches on the market.

Filip is a perfect Peacock. People search for his product by name, not by category. This is the true mark of a very rare bird.

So, which of these three animals most appeals to you?

Naturally, everyone gravitates toward the Peacock story at the end, but very few Peacocks ever grow as large as Filip. I also want to emphasize I personally have many friends who are very well fed Monkeys making a small fortune on Amazon by out-witting less active Lions and Peacocks.

Before you begin, you really need to search your heart and truly answer the question, "What kind of animal am I?"

For me, I am a Peacock. My Amazon brands are built on almost exactly the same principles as Filip's. I avoid super-competitive microclimates where Monkey's rule the roost. I avoid mega-categories like toothpaste, shaving cream, toilet paper and paper napkins because those are where Lions rule.

What I look for are products where travelers are prepared to dig in a little and search the jungle for the products they like, because the product they are buying isn't all about the price, or all about a marketing message (which Monkey's are great at).

I like to sell things where design matters. Thing people are going to put on display in their homes, use in front of their friends, or give as a gift. How these things *look* says something about who they are, whereas nobody is judging you for the Vitamin C pill you take or the paper towel you use to mop up your kitchen mess.

Is this starting to make sense?

So let me give you a quick summary of Lion traits, Monkey traits and Peacock traits.

LIONS

- Interested in the most highly trafficked areas of the jungle where most of the food is.

- Live in areas of the jungle where travelers repeatedly come back for the same products. Think consumable items like toilet paper, dish washing liquid, toothpaste, paper towels, and laundry detergent. The biggest Lion in the world is Proctor & Gamble. Visit them at www.us.pg.com/our-brands and you'll see the most famous Lion in history.

- Very well-funded and able to choke out any monkeys by simply dropping their prices to almost free if they have to. They are extremely territorial when it comes to the biggest feeding grounds and will lose money for as long as it takes to rid their microclimates of any monkeys making too much noise.

- Are not interested in fads or trends. They want to sell stuff people are always going to need.

- Are not interested in risky products making claims that may or may not be lived-up to. Think diet pills or fat loss creams.

MONKEYS

- Are master salespeople. They write great headlines and great sales copy.

- Are phenomenal analysts. They spend hours researching keywords and optimizing every aspect of their listings.

- Extremely creative when it comes to marketing. They will use coupons, create excellent follow-up email sequences, and drive traffic to their Amazon listing from other jungles like Facebook and Google.

- Are not as focused on the quality of the product because they are such good sales people they create the illusion of a great product by virtue of their marketing skills.

- Are easily distracted by shiny objects and always looking for the newest trend or hack to cash in on.

- Not afraid to sell products making claims which may or may not be lived-up to.

PEACOCKS

- Are focused on creating better products first, and how to market them second. Think Apple. Apple made a better machine with better software. The product *is* the marketing.

- Spend a lot of time thinking about exactly who, within the travelers passing through, in their microclimates, is *their* customer. They don't try to appeal to everyone.

- Spend a lot of time on one-time tasks like product development, their logo, packaging, and photography.

- Are drawn to stable markets where travelers will always be found. Like Lions, they are not into trends or fashions. They are rarely found trying to compete in consumable products like those the Lions love.

Setting Lions aside (because most people reading this book will never be a Lion), the most successful Amazon sellers are Monkey/ Peacock hybrids. This is true outside of Amazon as well. In the context of Amazon though, these hybrid creatures are actually rarer than you'd think.

The reason this is the case, is that tens of thousands of new Amazon sellers have bought courses on how to sell on Amazon from Monkeys: people who are pure marketers who told them they could make lots of money quickly, if only they learn these relatively simple Monkey skills (which actually aren't that simple).

The reason I am naturally drawn to being a Peacock, is that the older I get, the less I want to jump around from branch-to-branch, competing for vines with Red-Bull-Infused primates. I'm getting far too lazy for that! I'd rather potter away in the background for 6-12 months, finding and developing a really beautiful product, and then let the travelers find me without all the constant exertion of energy.

Please understand that like all things in life and business, these characterizations are rarely absolute and there are always exceptions.

Sometimes there are brands with the perfect synthesis of Monkey and Peacock. These brands may become a Lion, or be purchased by one. A great example is Dollar Shave Club. If you don't know the brand, go to YouTube and search "Dollar Shave Club".

Although not launched on Amazon, their story holds many valuable lessons.

These guys went into pure Lion territory, selling men's-shavers under a monthly subscription model. Their marketing was exceptional. Their branding was great and their product was awesome. Not only that, they were right in their estimation that the Lions had been feasting on too healthy a margin for too long in that healthy microclimate. $30 for a pack of five blades? Come on!

In short, Dollar Shave Club saw an opportunity to steal some of the Lion's food and they did it in a big way through the success of one hilarious video that went viral (the one I mentioned above).

Within three years, Unilever bought out Dollar Shave Club for $1 Billion in cash. Happy days!

It's important you aren't stuck in identifying yourself as one of the extremes. Jungles are eco-systems having all kinds of creatures that survive because of different incarnations and qualities, depending on the microclimate in which they live. On Amazon, those microclimates are very real and very subtle. Let me give you an example.

Many new Amazon sellers naturally gravitate towards things about which they are passionate. Let's say that thing is coffee.

If we wander over to that section of the jungle, we are going to find all kinds of microclimates where different things matter, depending on which particular area of the coffee terrain you are.

What matters if you're selling coffee *beans* is very different to what matters if you're selling a coffee *press*. What matters if you're selling a coffee *press* is vastly different to what matters if you're selling novelty coffee *cups*.

Each product lives in a different microclimate where different skills and assets are required to stand out, convert, get good reviews, and thrive long-term. This is because each product comes with a unique set of expectations from the customer, and the customers vary even within the same type of product.

Let's dig into that for a moment.

If you were buying coffee beans, what would matter most to you?

First, as a seller, if you're new in this space you are going to have to have strong Peacock skills concerning your logo and branding (one-time efforts attracting customers for life).

You want this logo and coffee bag to *look* amazing right out of the gate, because you'll be competing with some pretty clever coffee Peacocks who have spent a lot of time and money arranging their feathers (brand) to appeal to a particular section of the coffee drinking travelers passing through that highly trafficked section of the jungle. However, as amazing as the logo and bag needs to *look*, what really matters is how the coffee *tastes*.

You see, even if you make a great brand, and apply the skills of a master Monkey (great headlines, sales copy and other Monkey strategies I'll teach you later in this book), if you get a bunch of customers to a good-looking but bad-tasting coffee, all you'll end up doing is selling a lot of coffee to people who will soon leave you 1-star reviews. No Monkey in the world can sell a product on Amazon infected with bad reviews, no matter how good the logo or bag is.

So, now let's take a look at selling a coffee *press*.

What matters to coffee press buyers?

Well, first we need to take a close look at those travelers. Are they all the same? Does *everyone* want a cheap coffee press, or is there some variance there? How important is design to each of them? How important is where it's from? How important is the sustainability of the manufacture process?

In short, who are these travelers and what matters to them?

I am no coffee press expert, but my experience tells me that what you will find a range of travelers that go from the ramen-noodle-eating college kids, to the Silicon Valley coffee snobs who want (and can afford) the coolest looking, most sustain-ably produced coffee press known to man.

One traveler might pay $100 for their coffee press while the other is prepared to go all the way up to $12.99.

If you don't know *whom* you are targeting before you begin, how can you source a product, create a logo, or know what to spend on packaging?

Remember, before you gravitate to one end of these extremes or the other, there could be a lovely meal in the middle. Think Dollar Shave Club.

Dollar Shave Club weren't competing in the plastic shaver market, and they weren't charging $30 for five blades either. Instead, they used their outstanding Monkey and Peacock skills to create a product that looked like a $30 pack of Gillette blades, but provide them for $10/month and saved you, the customer, the hassle of having to go get them by mailing the blades to you each month. They also made us laugh in the process by poking fun at the Lions! As a result, they made a Billion dollars and became rich PeaMonkeys!

Is this starting to make sense?

Both the challenge and the opportunity on Amazon is in finding microclimates where there's enough travelers to feed you, and where the Lions aren't too vicious (or not there at all), while the Monkeys are *just* that - Monkeys.

Find those climates and you can build a very nice business indeed.

CHAPTER 4

★★★★★

PRIVATE LABELING

There are many ways to make money in the Amazon jungle, but what I teach is a concept called 'Private Labeling'. Private labeling refers to the common practice of putting your own label (or brand name) onto a product already manufactured somewhere in the world. Once made, the product is branded with your logo. You then control it, and nobody can undercut you on price because you are the only seller of that brand in the world.

Think about the coffee bean example I shared earlier. I am pretty sure sourcing coffee beans wouldn't be too difficult. You could sit down, think about the travelers that visit the coffee bean section of the jungle, and create an amazing logo and packaging (brand) focusing on the traveler type you want to attract.

Next, you find the suppliers and you taste-test all the various beans by soliciting the opinions of the snobbiest coffee drinkers you can find. People who live, breathe, and worship coffee. Once you reach a professional consensus, you are now in great shape to start your own 'Private Label' coffee brand.

Make sense?

This same strategy is applicable across almost any type of product. Sporting goods, home-wares, electronics, you name it, can be private labeled. I'll get to where you find suppliers in a moment.

The downside of private labeling is you actually have to buy the products from a manufacturer upfront. This means you have to invest real money into launching your company. It's a bummer, I know, but remember, by doing this, you own the brand and as your business grows, the value of your brand accrues to you and not someone else. Let me illustrate what I mean by explaining another Amazon strategy.

Another common strategy for making money on Amazon is 'drop-shipping'. Rather than creating your own brand and investing your own money into buying inventory, you simply find a supplier of something you want to sell, who already has the stock, and you sell their stuff on Amazon for them.

When you make a sale, you order the product from that supplier at a wholesale rate, and then you (or they) send it out, keeping whatever profit margin you managed to make in the middle.

Obviously, drop-shipping is a very attractive model from a risk point-of-view, because you don't have to risk your own capital to get started. You simply make money being an intermediary. If you know what you're doing, you can do quite well, but you'll always be a salesman and not a real business owner.

Business owners have control, and they build something they can sell. It's very hard to sell a business where your supplier, who owns the actual brand, could easily set up shop on Amazon right alongside you, or withdraw their permission for you to sell their stuff once they see how successful you've become (and they'll know because they're supplying you!).

For these reasons, I strongly encourage people to start their own private label brands because I earnestly believe it's the wisest way to create real wealth through selling physical products.

Later in this book, I will go into greater detail about how to research for product ideas, but for now, I want to talk about how to actually find a supplier, assuming you already have the product in mind.

These days, finding suppliers is relatively easy to do. The first place to start is online using sites like alibaba.com. This website is a directory of suppliers from all over the world who manufacture almost anything.

It is a Chinese website but it's owned by Alibaba Group, a publicly traded company which was (at least as I write this book), the highest valued company ever to be taken public. In short, it's a massive business catering exceptionally well to the millions of western business owners who use the site to find suppliers.

The second way to find suppliers is to physically attend a trade show or supplier market, most likely in China.

Again, this is where it all gets nuanced.

If you're going to sell supplements or face creams, then you probably won't go outside of the US. If you're going to sell coffee, then China is probably not the place to go either. It all depends on what you're going to sell. For the purposes of this chapter, I am going to assume that, like almost everything these days, your product will be made in China.

So let's begin with AliBaba.

As mentioned earlier, Alibaba is a global directory of wholesalers and manufacturers. You can find someone who makes just about anything there. Need 10,000 rubber ducks? No problem.

In just a few seconds, you can find out that rubber ducks cost between 10c and $2, depending on the style and quantity that you want.

What about something else? How about toy rocket launchers? A quick search will reveal that a "Stomp Rocket" is available for between $1 and $2.50, depending on how many you buy.

You can spend hours and hours just tumbling down rabbit holes on Alibaba, looking at the most random things you can imagine. What you quickly realize is just how much margin there is in almost everything you buy in the west.

If you keep Alibaba open on your computer and then go searching for the exact same item on Amazon in a new browser tab, you'll quickly see those rubber ducks that you can buy for between 10c and $2 on Alibaba, selling on Amazon for between $6 and $10. Assuming a $1 purchase price, that's a 600%-1,000% markup.

Those "Stomp Rockets" that cost between $1 and $2.50? They sell for $16 with just three rockets on Amazon. Assuming a $2 purchase price, that's an 800% markup!

Yes, there are other costs, but can you see how easy it is to establish whether or not there's a profit margin to be made?

Ok, so let's talk about how to use Alibaba like an expert so you can filter your results and separate good suppliers from the average (or worse).

If you look at the left hand edge of the page where any search results are displayed, you'll see you can filter your results by general location, country, and then region. In addition to geographical filters, you can also filter them by what quality verifications they have. You can then choose to see only suppliers with any, all, or a combination of the following:

- Trade Assured

- Gold Suppliers

- Onsite checked

- Assessed

Let's take a peek at what each of these criteria mean.

First, "Trade Assured" means you can make all payments through Alibaba, rather than making payments to the supplier directly. In other words, you are using Alibaba as an escrow agent who will only release funds to the supplier when particular milestones are met. Obviously, only suppliers that are really going to supply you the goods will agree to use Trade Assurance. It's a way of them showing you they are prepared to keep their word and only be paid when they deliver what is promised.

The second kind of quality filter is "Gold Supplier". Technically, this level of status has no direct benefit to you as a buyer on its own. The suppliers pay Alibaba a premium level membership to join which enables them access to

better tools and other verifications that help them stand out to buyers (like you) on their site.

The Gold Supplier status has no direct benefit to you. Only Gold Suppliers can apply for the "Onsite Check" verification status explained below.

The third filter is "Onsite Check" - only available to Gold Suppliers. This filter is really useful and one of my favorites. Suppliers with this status have paid Alibaba to send one of their employees out to their factory to verify they actually do exist, and they have all necessary licenses in place to operate their business in compliance with Chinese law.

The final filter is the "Assessed Supplier". I also really love this one. The main difference between this status and "Onsite Checked" is an independent assessment company carries out the assessment and not Alibaba.

Now these are not some "rinky-dink" (and slightly sketchy) inspection companies. These global inspection firms aren't easily bribed. Amongst others, they are responsible for the following:

- Check the company's legal status
- Check the company's address
- Verify the company's production capacity
- Verify the company's export revenue and main clients
- Verify where the company distributes
- Verify the company does have a research & development (R&D) team
- Check whether the company has design staff and the appropriate equipment

What's really cool is that these inspectors produce downloadable reports and publish videos shot on site for you to see the factory *before* you do business. This is a high level of verification as it sifts the middlemen and brokers from the real manufacturers.

I can instantly see a video of the factory as well as a bunch of photos. I can determine how many employees they have as well as the locations of their top export markets. This is fantastic info that not all manufacturers can offer.

The next awesome thing you should know about is AliSourcePro. This, too, is free, and it enables you to post what you're looking for and how many units you're after while suppliers come to you instead of you spending hours digging around.

At the time of writing this book, the service is available at: sourcing.alibaba.com

The URLs do change, so if you have any issue, just Google "AliSourcePro" and you'll find it.

All you have to do is select whether you're a buyer or a seller and then create what's called an "RFQ". "RFQ" is an acronym for "Request For Quotation". From there you simply follow the prompts, and within a few minutes, you'll have suppliers submitting bids manageable from right inside Alibaba.

The truth is, I could write a completely separate book just on finding and dealing with suppliers through Alibaba, but that's not what this book is about. So rather than do that, I'm going to focus on just two things and then talk to you about travelling to China, attending trade shows, and other buying locations.

So here's the two things I want to teach you:

1. Buy your competitors' products on Amazon *before* you start sourcing on Alibaba.

2. Don't look for the cheapest supplier. Look for the *best* supplier. They are rarely the same thing but the cheapest one can sink your business.

Let's begin with buying your competitor's product on Amazon first. This may be one of the smartest things you do. It lowers your risk and improves your own product offering. It can also save you a ton of money while giving you incredibly valuable data that lazy and cheap entrepreneurs never acquire. Buying your competitor's stuff almost always turns up a lot of great information and ideas that you can use and learn from.

You'll discover things like:

- How their packaging looks and feels in real life
- What their product is actually like to use
- What's good and bad about their design
- What email follow up they do (usually none)
- Whether or not they put anything inside of their boxes to build a relationship or ask you to buy something else from them

All this information is *extremely* useful to have when you're about to start designing your product and talking to manufacturers.

Is the handle too thin? Does the packaging feel cheap? Is the stitching really of a low quality? Is the zipper too light? Is there a fundamental design flaw? Does the color rub off? Does it break in a dishwasher? Does the chord keep falling out? Does the lid wobble? Is the base too light?

You will be amazed at how differently you analyze a product when you're about to buy 1,000 of them for $10,000 as opposed to one of them for $10! You will also be shocked at how many things can go wrong on even the simplest of items.

So now you've bought four or five of your competitor's products on Amazon and you know what you do and don't want. Now you're ready to submit your first RFQ on AliSourcePro.

When it comes to doing these RFQs, my advice is to slow down, be clear, and don't make yourself sound cheap or small. Chinese suppliers are bombarded all day, every day, with rude, complacent, and aloof Westerners making ill-thought-through RFQ requests.

If you take your time and put together a professional brief of what you want, what your quality standards are, and what kind of relationship you're looking to build long term, you're going to attract the attention of the better suppliers.

This isn't rocket science, but most people are lazy and have no standards. This gives you an opportunity to shine! As a rule of thumb, a good RFQ may take a couple of hours to put together, not a few minutes.

Other things to keep in mind…

Chinese suppliers are not poor, stupid, or your servant. Just like you, they are looking to make a profit and build a good business, preferably working with people they don't despise.

Once you start getting bids back, I want you to really pay attention to the entire experience of dealing with each supplier. Try as best as you can to minimize the price element of the quotes, and think about the whole experience, including:

- How is their English?
- How quickly did they respond?
- How well written is their email to you?
- How focused are they on quality versus price?
- Are they verified on Alibaba?

These subtle things actually matter a lot more than the price at this stage.

This is really easy to read and agree with while you're sitting in your armchair reading this book, but most of us have deep-seated issues around money. When we start getting quotes back for those rubber ducks, all of our logic can fly out of the window as our inner "Scrooge McDuck" kicks in! Even the best of us can become fiercely focused on dollars and cents and blind to the overall experience of the company.

If you remember only one thing, remember this.

You get what you pay for.

Sure, this is not always true, but it's true enough that it won't hurt you as a starting point when you're going into a new product negotiation. Never forget you are never going to have as much experience with rubber ducks as the person who's been making millions of them for years. So don't act like the rubber duck expert when you're not, or you're going to look like a rubber *dick* in record time.

Rather than assuming that one supplier is ripping you off because they quoted 85c and the other guy only quoted 35c, seek to understand *why*, and take the position that, generally speaking, there will be a reason.

Just remember these ducks sell for between $6 and $10 on Amazon and 50c/unit is not going to break you, but having a duck that sinks because the rubber stopper falls out and the bath water turns yellow when all the dye runs off will! What are you going to do with the remaining 934 little rubber ducks when someone writes a review that alleges your little duck sinks and pees in the bath?

The biggest risk on Amazon is having a product that generates many poor reviews. Once this happens, you are dead in the water and you'll have to begin the painful task of liquidating your inventory and trying to recover your capital to start again. At best, you will lose months of effort and research, all because your lizard brain took over, and you ignored the common sense rules of good duck buying!

One tip I give all of my students about buying in China is asking your favorite bidders what they could do to the product if you were prepared to pay 20% more for your rubber duck than the price they have quoted you.

Wait. What?

You heard me right! Ask them what they could improve if you paid 20% *more* than their asking price. You'll be both amazed and amused at the mixed responses you get.

First of all, before your lizard brain freaks out, remember that on a $5 item we are talking about a $1 difference. In almost every case, this $1 bump is easily recoverable by simply adding $1 (or more) to the higher quality product at the retail end.

In many cases, though, you can charge substantially *more* than the small premium you paid at the wholesale end, and sometimes the $1 extra investment will redefine your product entirely.

As a basic rule of thumb, you need to be selling the product on Amazon at five times more than a supplier is quoting you on Alibaba. So a $5 item should have a retail price of around $25. If you pay $6 for a substantially better product, could you charge $27.50 or even $30 for it at the retail end?

The $1 invested at the manufacture point might earn you $2.50 or $5 extra at market. That's between 2.5X and 5X return on your $1 investment, and you get a product more likely to get awesome reviews because it's actually better. Oh, and you get less complaints, a better brand reputation and a life free of stress.

Makes sense, right?

Aside from all these benefits, the 20% offer will surprise and delight your Chinese supplier and elevate you from the arrogant swarm of rude Westerners. Once you clearly explain you're not like most Western buyers (who expect the best from the least amount of money), and you have a long term vision for your company built on trust and quality, they'll start to think about how they can make you the best rubber-ducky in the business.

You are winning friends and influencing people by aligning their interests with your own, using the one thing that speaks all languages - money.

Over the last few years, I've gotten to know all kinds of Amazon sellers, from small players making a few thousand dollars a year, right up to mega-sellers who do seven figures a month. Almost without exception, those sellers who have been around for a while cite their relationship with their supplier as the #1 most important thing in their business.

Once the nerves and negotiations are done on the first order, if you're lucky, you have years ahead of you. Just remember that you will be dealing with someone on the other side of the world who is *absolutely critical* to your long-term success. No supplier = no business.

OK, so let's now talk about trade shows and visiting China to meet suppliers first hand.

The most famous trade show in China is the Canton Fair. It runs twice a year, once in April and once in October. The show is free to attend and held in Guangzhou, which is in the south of China, not far from Hong Kong. Most westerners fly into Hong Kong, and travel by train from Hong Kong to Guangzhou.

The show has three phases. Phase 1 is Electronics and Household Tools. Phase 2 is Home-ware and Gifts. Phase 3 is

Office, Textiles, Health and Medical products. The official website for this fair is http://www.cantonfair.org.cn

The first thing to be prepared for is simply how big the place is. It's a bit like going to the Las Vegas strip. In Vegas, you quickly learn the hotels are a lot further apart than they appear, because the scale of everything is massive. You could walk for what feels like an hour, only to discover you've only gone past three hotels!

On a practical level, my advice is to take running shoes to China and be prepared for several days of work and walking. This is not a place to go for a holiday.

A few other pointers you should be aware of…

In China, at least as I write this book, Google, Facebook, and many other social media platforms are blocked. Therefore, if you're a Gmail user and social media is part of your life, you're going to need what's called a VPN on your cell phone and laptop computer in order to access these services during your stay in China.

A really good one you can sign up for on a month-to-month subscription is www.expressvpn.com. It has a smart phone app as well as desktop version for Mac or PC device.

What a VPN does is change the IP address location on your computer or smart phone when going online. In other words, the Chinese Government won't see your device as accessing the internet from inside of China, but rather the US or whatever country you choose when turning on the VPN software.

It's much easier than it sounds and pretty much all Westerners use a VPN in China.

The recommendation is making sure that you have data on your mobile devices in order to connect to the Internet from wherever you are in China. Don't rely on the WIFI networks at hotels, coffee shops and conference centres.

The biggest benefit of being connected is being able to check how a product you are looking at might fare in relation to similar products already selling on Amazon, right there on the spot. If you're looking at flashing LED dog collars and the supplier wants $2 a unit, having mobile allows you to jump on Amazon right there on the spot to see what they're selling for and how crowded that particular microclimate is. You can quickly assess how many Monkeys, Peacocks and Lions are doing business and how well they're doing it. This is priceless, but only if you have access! Don't miss this tip!

The next thing to know is you need to obtain a visa to visit China. I won't bog you down in details now, but one tip, which may be helpful, is it's usually easier to get a tourist visa than a business visa, so you might decide to go that route the first time you decide to go to China.

My other two key travel tips for business trips to China are:

1. Have a business card.
2. Set up an email address that is used only on this business card and not used for anything else.

In China, business cards are widely used and you'll be asked for yours frequently when talking to suppliers. That being said, the Chinese generally don't care *at all* about standard email etiquette, especially as it relates to privacy. It's not uncommon that they'll sell or rent your name and email address. You'll then learn the true meaning of spam and how poorly the word "unsubscribe" translates in Chinese. So be mindful of this, otherwise you'll be hearing about rubber ducks, Stomp Rockets, and all manner of things you casually looked at whilst in China until the day you die.

OK, so from a purely business perspective, why go to China and not just find suppliers online.

Here are some things about finding suppliers online….

First, finding suppliers online is a singular experience. You've probably looked at a relatively tiny sector of the retail landscape, and you've zeroed in on a micro-sector of one tiny niche - a singular product. It's a bit like looking for a Mars bar supplier only, rather than getting a private tour of Willy Wonka's entire Chocolate Factory and then deciding what you want to sell. It's hard to describe the many benefits of the immersive experience of the latter versus the digital experience of the former. Simply put, like most things in life, nothing beats being there in person!

Aside from the experiential benefits, where you'll save time is in sampling and development. When you're starting out, you'll ask a supplier at some point to send you a sample. If you go the online only route, you'll probably spend weeks (or months) going through RFQs, negotiating on price and other details, and then you'll finally get samples from three or four suppliers.

Now let's contrast that with going to the Canton Fair in person...

You can literally meet 20 suppliers of the same product in a single day. You can touch their samples and talk about how you'd like them tweaked right there on the spot. Not only that, but you'll actually experience how good their English is, you'll see how they operate, and you'll get a sense of who they are in a much more meaningful way than if you're just looking at an Excel spreadsheet with a tiny photo on it.

But it doesn't stop here. While you're at their stand, they'll more than likely have their entire product catalogue printed out and ready to give to you. Unlike the digital approach where you ask them about a single product and they send you a single quote, they'll give you access to their entire Chocolate Factory and show you everything they make in their catalogue.

You'll no doubt find a bunch of other products that might make a nice starter set of "Amazon houses" to stake your claim on the Amazon monopoly board. Who knows, you may even stumble across a hotel in disguise!

Seriously, this idea of starting with five products (houses) rather than one is really smart, because no matter how smart you think you are, you will always be surprised about what does well on Amazon and what doesn't.

I remember ordering four new products from my supplier once. At the last minute she showed me one other product and said to me, "I think this will do really well."

Thankfully, I wasn't too stuck on my own opinion. I agreed to take 1,000 units even though I didn't think much of the product. I put it on Amazon. It was an instant hotel, producing 5X more than any of my other Amazon houses were producing. Today, this product (that I missed) makes me six figures a year!

The other big thing you get by travelling to China is the opportunity to meet the experts and learn at hyper-speed. Who else do you know has spent years of their lives making rubber ducks, Stomp Rockets, or children's dinner plates? What you can learn by listening to the advice of people who have been making and exporting these products for years is immeasurable, especially when it's your first time at the rodeo.

So the message here is simple. By going to China, you expose yourself to an amount of learning and idea generation that is almost impossible to replicate by staying at home and trying to figure it out by yourself.

If going to the Canton Fair doesn't work because of timing, you can visit Yiwu, a year round trade fair based in the city of Yiwu, about two hours (by plane) north of Guangzhou. At the time of writing this book, there are several daily flights between these two destinations. You may even want to do both fairs whilst in the region.

My last piece of advice about going to these fairs is the following. If possible, spend the extra money to stay at hotels located next to or very near to the fair. When I go to the Canton Fair, I always stay at either the Langham or the Shangri-La, both of which are directly opposite the show. They're not cheap (especially during show time), but the last thing you're going to feel like doing is fighting Guangzhou traffic or catching trains when you've been walking all day at the Canton Fair. You'll just want to fall into bed or do your research in the hotel room. If possible, spend the money on being close to the fair so you preserve energy and focus on business. It will pay off big time when you're in a place like China.

At the end of the day, sourcing products and exporting from China is exciting, challenging, and hugely rewarding if you get it right. It is not something that will be amazing the first time. If, however, you persist and learn from the right people you will get much better at it over time.

If all of this is starting to make sense, and you want more training on the matter, feel free to visit my website at www.reliable. education and enroll in my free Amazon course.

Take a look at our blog and you'll see various posts I've made from all over the world. In several of them, I take you inside some of my supplier's factories in China and I show you the scale and excitement of Chinese mass manufacturing in full swing.

CHAPTER 5

★ ★ ★ ★ ★

BRAND **BUILDING**
BASICS

Brands - what are they and why are they important on Amazon?

Here's the thing…

In order to create a brand in a world where products are easily copied or imitated, you must focus on the details making up the whole *experience* of buying from you. Watches, for example, are easy to source, but selling them for $50,000 (or more) like Rolex does is something only a few brands have managed.

So why is that?

What is it about a Rolex that make people willing to pay so much more?

In my lifetime, I've purchased two Rolexes. One was for me while the other was a gift for one of my business partners. The first one I purchased was in Vienna, Austria. I was doing really well with one of my companies, and I'd taken my girlfriend for a surprise trip to Europe.

As we stood outside the Rolex dealership on a cold Austrian morning, looking at what would have been several million dollars worth of watches on display, we could see the impeccably dressed salespeople quietly showing watches to well-heeled customers inside.

The window display itself was something to behold. The glass panels were impeccably clean, and each window frame was thick gold. Nothing about the display looked cheap or cluttered.

As we moved towards the entrance, we could see a big security guard inside. Like the other staff, he, too, was elegantly dressed and nothing about him made you scared, but you did have a sense that if it came down to it, you would be fairly unsuccessful in trying to steal a Rolex in that particular store.

Once at the door, we had to push a small security button, silently alerting the staff that we would like to come inside and take the next step.

Before I tell you what happened next, I want you to think about the *context* already created. We hadn't touched a watch, we hadn't set foot in their store, but they had already told us so much about their brand and what owning a Rolex means. As it turns out, we humans are incredibly susceptible to suggestion.

If you go into a picture-framing store inside of your local shopping mall, and there's framed paintings stacked up 15 deep and leaning against the wall, what is your assumption about the value of those paintings? What context has been created?

Compare that with walking into a high-ceiling, all white, art gallery, with 10 paintings on display, each given their own oversized white wall and several dedicated spotlights to display them. What's your assumption now?

"These paintings must be insanely expensive!"

Right?

Put a creative-looking, immaculately dressed, trendy eyeglass wearing man or women in the corner and you increase the perceived value of the art again.

Simply put, context matters.

So how on earth does this relate to selling products on Amazon, a place where there are neither stores nor staff? I'll get to that in a moment, but for now, let's get back to the Rolex store on that crisp morning in Vienna.

As soon as we walked inside, the Security Guard swung around to face us, and, with a serene and welcoming smile, he said, "Welcome to Rolex". He then gestured toward the display counters where sales staff were waiting.

As we slowly walked toward the counters, a quiet sense of occasion came over me. I was just about to begin the process of buying what had been a massive goal of mine since my first Tony Robbins seminar when I was 19 years old.

The immaculately dressed and articulate Austrian gentleman that served us that day couldn't have been nicer.

"Would you two care for some hot chocolate or perhaps a tea?"

The brand experience was now in full swing.

Pretty soon, we were sitting in a small private room at the back of the store with our salesperson and his assistant who brought us hot chocolate and handmade Austrian pastries, which, apparently, came from a local baker a few blocks away.

Over the next half an hour, I tried on about a half a million dollars worth of Rolex watches and was having the time of my life. Despite me being a 27 year old kid from Australia, they didn't make me feel like I didn't belong or Rolex was beyond me.

You probably know how the rest of the story goes, but there is so much to be learned from this Rolex brand experience if only you slow down enough to notice the details. Everything from the elegant logo, to the luxurious, oversized boxes each watch is presented in, to the way the staff are dressed and watches displayed - is all part of the brand experience.

Rolexes are not just watches. They are an exclusive club with a membership card that tells the time.

Herein lays the subtle yet powerful mindset that all great product creators have. They care deeply about the details.

While some Amazon sellers will tell you this story is overkill when it comes to selling products on Amazon, let me tell you a true story of how I experienced a micro-degree of this level of brand respect by virtue of my brand name, the packaging I created, and the photos I had done on one of my Amazon brands.

I don't publicly reveal what I sell on Amazon because I don't want every other want-to-be Amazon seller to copy me, but let's just say I sell high end products for the home.

Before entering the market, I took time to think about who the travelers were in that microclimate and decided to go after the higher end consumers among them. I also took a careful look at my competition. I looked at:

- How well they named themselves
- How good their logo was
- How well they had written their product descriptions
- How beautiful their packaging was
- How much attention they paid to their product photography
- Where they had priced themselves in the market

My research revealed mostly average listings that had been put up by a new type of creature that I haven't yet identified in this book - Sloths. Sloths simply have no business being on Amazon, yet remarkably, there are still microclimates where Sloths are doing well because neither the Monkeys nor Peacocks have found them yet!

So there I was, in a microclimate full of Sloths and a few lazy Lions, and I entered with:

- A luxurious sounding name
- A killer logo
- World class packaging
- Stunning photos
- Articulate product messaging
- A price lower than the famous Lion brands, but much more than the Sloths

Guess what happened?

If you guessed it went bananas, you guessed right.

I hit it out of the park.

But here's the really awesome part. Since then, Amazon has launched its own brand against me and the microclimate has become flooded by Chinese suppliers who sell very similar looking items at half my price or less – but without my brand and packaging.

I'm *still* doing great.

In fact, not long ago, I received an email from a lady in the UK who wanted to verify the proper weight of the product she'd purchased from me. It was a strange question and one I'd never heard before.

When I inquired as to why she wanted to verify the weight she explained:

"Times have been bit tough so I've decided to sell the product I bought from you. I put it on eBay, a guy came around, and he too is a fan of your brand. He has several of your products and thought mine was a fake because he didn't think it was heavy enough."

I was floored.

First of all, until that moment, I hadn't thought there would be a secondhand market for my products at all. Secondly, I couldn't believe people had imagined there could be fake versions of my product.

My name, logo, packaging and photography, combined with my very classy follow up email sequences had created an *experience* that created a brand.

At that moment, I knew I was a successful PeaMonkey!

In the first paragraph of this chapter, I said this:

"In order to create a brand in a world where products are easily copied or imitated, you must focus on the details making up the whole experience of buying from you."

Sloths and Lions don't think about this stuff. Sloths are too lazy and most Lions are too big and slow. Monkeys and Peacocks focus on these things because they know that's the only way they'll get a meal.

Please remember though, not every product has to go to the extreme that I did regarding packaging and naming. If you don't sell a product where having a fancy name and super expensive packaging works, then don't do those things. You'll simply overcapitalize or miss your market.

You have to assess each product in the context of the microclimate and the prevailing competitors who live there.

Therefore, before you get too excited about making an amazing "Rolex-like" brand, you really need to answer these questions:

- Does design play a significant part in the buying decision?
- Is the packaging important?
- How important are good photos?

- Do reviews matter a lot when making a decision to buy or not?

- Would you choose one product over another based on the description of it in the Amazon listing?

- Would people even read the written words in your listing before they buy, or are they most likely to buy just based on the photos and general review rating?

- How many pages deep into the search results are they likely to go before making a decision? If you sell napkins, shoppers will probably only look at the top five listings on page #1 (Lion territory for this kind of product), but for a men's watch they'll probably scroll several pages deep into the search results.

The answers to all of these questions will give you an idea of how important branding and design are, and how much of a Peacock or Monkey you're going to need to be.

Let me give you an example of how this type of thinking can be applied to even the simplest of products.

About three years ago, I was at a Yoga and meditation retreat on a tiny island off the coast of Bali. There was, in total, only five attendees. They were mainly stressed-out entrepreneurs and business people looking for more balance in their lives.

Jeremy was one of them - a super-nice guy from New Zealand. Jeremy had recently sold his adventure business and was looking for something new to do. His rules were simple: no employees and travel was a must.

Naturally, we started talking about Amazon. I showed him what I was selling and how much I was making, even while I was chilling out on the Indian Ocean, enjoying delicious Balinese food and Yoga on the beach. His mind was blown away.

Like all entrepreneurs, Jeremy immediately saw the power of the Amazon business model and decided there and then to get into it.

Jeremy started with three products, but I want to tell you about the first one because it perfectly illustrates my point about applying these "Rolex" principles, even if what you're selling is only $15.

Unlike me, Jeremy started with a product mostly selling for between $10-$14 on Amazon. To protect his hard work and privacy, I won't reveal what he sells, but I will say that it's a very small item (just a few ounces), and you can air freight 1,000 of them in a few small boxes. It doesn't break, it doesn't go out of date, and there's very little that can go wrong with it over time. It's a perfect Amazon product! Not only that, but the wholesale cost is less than $2/unit so you can start *really* cheaply.

So how on earth do you "Rolex" that kind of thing?

Well, after carefully studying the microclimate, Jeremy figured out some pretty interesting things about the travelers, and *why* they were buying that item. He figured out "the context", a word I have used a lot in this chapter.

The key insight Jeremy had, that others hadn't been aware of, was the fact people were buying these products as a gift or as part of a gift. With this in mind, Jeremy decided to invest just a few dollars into branding and packaging.

He created a cool name. He created a cool logo. He created a cool box. He took amazing photos. Later in this chapter, I'll reveal exactly where I get all that stuff done, so stay with me.

When Jeremy entered the market, his competitors weren't branding or packaging their products at all. They were simply putting the little item in a plastic bag and sending it out. Like most Sloths, they couldn't be bothered with branding, and, as it turns out, people *do* care about branding and packaging when they're gift giving.

Whereas his competitors' COGS (Cost Of Goods Sold) were probably only $2/unit, Jeremy's was $4/unit (double). Jeremy wasn't concerned because he felt, very strongly, that he could recover the extra $2 (and perhaps a little more) at the retail end and his hunch was right.

He opened on Amazon at just below the price of his main competitors, and within a month or two, he was #1 on Amazon for that product. Customers voted with their wallets and he won.

Today, Jeremy has been able to slide his price up to $20/unit, much more expensive than his Sloth competitors, and he is still at #1 because people not only want branding in this microclimate, they're prepared to pay for it.

Like I said, this is not true for each microclimate, but it is for many. That's the research you have to do. Jeremy found a microclimate where branding matters and no Peacock or a Lion is in sight!

Today, this one little item earns Jeremy about USD $700/day in sales, just from selling in the US. That's a whopping $255,000/year at about a 40% profit margin.

What if he now opens into more than 30 other countries like I have? He just has to ship some of his products to Amazon's warehouses in Europe, open a seller account there, port his listing information across, and he's in business and making Pounds, Euros and all kinds of other currency!

Another amazing thing is that you can, quite often, find products that are already well branded and well packaged on the floor at the Canton Fair in China. Yes, there are Chinese Peacocks too, but Peacocks that never go into retail. What if you can find something like that and all you have to do is change the logo?

Here's the thing about success...

As Woody Allen says, "80% of success is showing up."

You have to be in the game and doing the work to find these opportunities. Thankfully, most people want them *given* to them. I say "thankfully" because this level of laziness thins out the herd of real competitors.

Before I finish this chapter, let me give you a few tips on how I actually get this branding stuff done. Contrary to what you're probably thinking, I don't do any of this myself. I understand the concept and then I hire experts to do the work.

Here's what I mean…

First, I almost never name any product, business or project that I'm working on myself. Instead, I crowd-source my names by using a naming website called Squad Help. You can find them at www.squadhelp.com

Squad Help is a website that has 1000's of creative people around the world who all compete to win your naming contest. I usually offer about $300 to come up with a name for my product, book, or company, and I get about 800 names to choose from. Depending on what it is you're trying to name, you can even request only names where the corresponding .com domain is available too. It's fascinating!

This book was actually named via a contest I ran there. How perfect is the name "Primed" for a book about Amazon? I think it's brilliant but I cannot take credit for it.

I am, every time I use the site, blown away by how much thought these people put into naming things. I imagine they are the type of people who love crossword puzzles and Jeopardy. They have an entire part of the human brain I think God skipped when putting me together!

With regards to logos, I use 99Designs.com. Just like Squad Help, this is a crowdsourcing service where you put up a graphic design contest. Designers from all over the world compete to win your prize.

My advice here is as follows:

1. Create an amazing brief. The more you tell the designers about the type of consumer you're trying to reach, and provide samples of logos you like, the better the result you're going to get.

2. Don't be cheap. Remember what I said about only getting what you pay for? Great designers don't work for small money.

3. Make the design contest "blind". This is a feature you may have to ask them to activate for you if it's your first contest. Essentially, it means the designers cannot see other people's work or your feedback on their designs as they are submitted. Good designers prefer these contests because they don't allow others to wait to see what you like, only to be copied by the less talented designers.

4. Be active in giving feedback and be patient. Designers hate nothing more than submitting work that is totally ignored by the contest organizer (you). They are giving you their time and ideas completely on spec. The least you can do is respond.

Also, the best designers often wait until the last day or two before submitting. This way they reduce the chances of being copied while increasing the impact of their entry because their entry is fresh in your mind as you approach the deadline.

In short, good designers know they're good and it's very rare that any of the first designs will be your winner. If you haven't been cheap, the good designers will come.

This book cover was actually designed on 99Designs as well. I paid $1,000 for it (which is really high for the marketplace), but I got great designers and this designer was one of the last to enter.

My final tip is to get *amazing* photos. For that, I use www.seller-photo.com. It is a company I, together with one of my business partners, Keith O'Brien, own.

After years of seeing online retailers trying to sell products with sub-standard photography, I decided to setup a company to help people out with that. Today, we take professional product photos for all kinds of sellers across almost every microclimate in the jungle!

To give you an idea of how focused the SellerPhoto.com team is, they hire the types of people who will sit with a product for 15 minutes, carefully studying every angle, looking for the engineering in even the simplest of products around.

One day, I walked into the creative room to find one of our creative directors staring at the plug on the end of an iPhone chord. So intent was her focus that I thought she must have taken Magic Mushrooms or smoked a joint when nobody was watching. She was transfixed by this chord.

For the record, our staff are *not* high, but her answer to my inquiry about what she was up to was awesome.

"These things are really amazing. There's quite a bit of engineering in them when you slow down enough and take a *real* look at them. I have found some great angles from which I am going to shoot this chord. I'm going to go super-close up and really showcase this engineering."

High-five Keith! These are the kinds of people I want obsessing over my products before taking photos of them. This is Peacock thinking to the extreme! Do you think that Monkeys think like this? Or Sloths?

Just remember, before you go down the rabbit hole, you have to ask the question, "Does branding and design matter in the microclimate in which I want to sell?"

If the answer is no, then you can disregard some of this chapter and get on with Monkey marketing and do well anyway!

If you sell napkins, branding and design don't matter that much. These are everyday consumable items that you literally throw in the trash after you're done.

If, on the other hand, you sell men's watches, yes, branding and design *do* matter. A watch is a personal item that says something about who you are, and you're going to be looking at it everyday for a few years.

Therefore, before you get all excited about making a brand, you really need to answer these questions:

- Does design play a significant part in the buying decision?
- Is the packaging important?

- How important are good photos? How well are your competitors doing that?

- Do reviews matter a lot when making a decision to buy or not?

- Would you choose one product over another based on the description of it in the Amazon listing?

- Would people even read the written words in your listing before they buy, or are they most likely to buy just based on the photos and general review rating?

- How many pages deep into the search results are they likely to go before making a decision? With napkins, they'll probably only look at the top five listings on page #1, but for a men's watch the answer is very different.

The answers to all of these questions will give you an idea of how important branding and design are, and how much of a Peacock or Monkey you're going to need to be.

Also, even if branding *does* matter, make sure you check on Amazon to see whether you'll stand out in the context of who's there already. There are some microclimates already overflowing with Peacocks (like watches), so even if you nail it, you may not have any real competitive advantage when taken to the market.

What you want is what Jeremy found - a microclimate where Peacock qualities do matter, but with few (if any) Peacocks there already.

Make sense?

I like branding because it requires more thought and more talent than just using cold, hard, marketing to sell products. Most people don't want to think, and most people don't want to work to become more talented in an area where 1 + 2 doesn't always equal 3. People like certainty rather than subtlety. Great branding requires curiosity, creativity, and objectivity.

That truth is what enables me to have a far less stressful life than the pure Monkeys. Monkeys know whilst it's not easy to become a great marketer, it is more common. Monkeys are everywhere because they've been selling courses to each other for years!

The subtle art of reading a marketplace and branding your products accordingly is not common because almost nobody teaches it. If you can develop this skill, just as Jeremy has, you're a rare bird indeed.

CHAPTER 6

★ ★ ★ ★ ★

WHAT **SHOULD** I SELL ON **AMAZON**?

Without doubt, the #1 question I am asked about Amazon is this:

"What should I sell?"

These are four simple words holding a vast majority of people back from ever starting an Amazon business.

If you want to avoid the mistake of letting not knowing what to sell stop you from getting started on Amazon, then do the following.

STEP #1

Go to www.aliexpress.com and buy a few cheap products from China. Seriously, do this right now.

Just buy 10 pairs of sunglasses, 10 candles, or 10 golf balls. It doesn't matter what you buy, so long as it's cheap and small (so you it can be shipped by air).

STEP #2

Open an Amazon Seller account. Just Google "open an Amazon seller central account" and you'll find the page easily. To start with, you can open a free account. Don't worry about what Amazon's fees are on the 10 products that you're going to sell. The point here is <u>not</u> to make money, it's to learn the really basic steps to exporting a product, opening an Amazon account, creating a listing, and then (hopefully), selling something.

Honestly, if you do this, you will learn way more than someone who spends $2,000 on a course but never actually exports anything or opens an Amazon seller account. While they're stuck worrying about what *might* happen, you're taking action and finding out for yourself (with very little risk).

The steps above should take all of 15 minutes to complete and will cost you less than $100. Why don't you go do it right now? Be an entrepreneur and not a "wantrepreneur". Take action!

Did you do it?

Your life is not changed through reading alone. It's changed through the *ACTIONS* you take.

I won't go anywhere. I'll be right here waiting when you get back.

For those of you who actually *did* as I suggested, WELL DONE!

You are in the 2% of people who actually take action. Often in business, it's that simple. The herd has already been thinned!

STEP #3

It's time to create a listing on Amazon once your products arrive (usually a few days later if shipped by air). This, too, is super simple.

Just log into your brand new Seller Central account, click on "Inventory" in the top left hand corner, AND then "Add A Product".

Now, depending on when you read this book, and the changes Amazon may make over time, the interface might change, but I'm sure you'll figure it out.

What you want to do is click on where it says, "Create A New Product Listing".

The next step is to choose a product category. Amazon makes it super easy by allowing you to enter some keywords. It will then search the category for you. Alternatively, you can manually select the category using Amazon's structure as laid out on that page.

Can you believe you are almost here and ready to start selling on Amazon?

STEP #4

Once you've selected the category you're going to be selling in, the next step is to create the actual listing. All this requires is for you to complete seven information tabs covering everything from the name of your product, to size and weight, where it's from, and so forth. You also upload your photos here.

This information is known as "meta-data", and it's what Amazon uses to know exactly what this item is. When people search for it, they know to include your product in the search results.

To summarize, the tabs are:

1. Vital Info

2. Variations

3. Offer

4. Images

5. Description

6. Keywords

7. More Details

Not too intimidating, is it?

Once you've chosen your product, these seven tabs are where you spend most of your time as an Amazon seller. Working on what goes in these tabs is mostly Monkey work, whereas everything you do *before* you get here is Peacock work.

In order to complete these seven tabs, you need the following eight criteria as a minimum.

1. A headline for your product

2. A set of five bullet points to describe the features of your product

3. A paragraph of sales copy to go into the description section of your Amazon listing

4. At least one photo of the product on a pure white background

5. Weight and dimensions of your product

6. List of keywords that people might search for in order to find your product

7. SKU code

8. Barcode

I am, in this book, not diving into each of these areas in depth as this book is a high-level overview of the Amazon business opportunity, not a detailed course delving into the ever-changing nuances of Monkey mastery.

For that kind of training, see my website at www.reliable.education

I give away a free course on the site to help you start and then if you want to do the full program and join our global community of students, you can do that as well.

For now, I want you to learn how to get the listing of your first product live, because once you've done that, you are way ahead of 98% of people who *think* about starting an Amazon business but never do!

If you go to Amazon and search for products similar to the one you're trying to list, you'll quickly get a sense of what's required for points 1-6. They don't have to be perfect right now, they just have to be complete.

The only slightly tricky pieces are the SKU and the barcode.

So let me talk about the SKU first.

The SKU is required in the first tab of the product setup. The SKU is simply a code you assign to the product for your internal reference or catalog. It can be anything you want. To keep it simple, I make up an acronym based on the product I'm selling.

For example, if I was selling tennis rackets, and the one I was selling was named "The Ace" (a brand name I just made up), then I might say the SKU for the "Ace Tennis Racket" is "ATR01".

Make sense?

The last piece of vital information you need is a barcode number. You can't just make these up. Once you have this barcode number, you will need to make actual barcodes using that number and attach it to each of your 10 items.

This is very important because when Amazon gets your products at the warehouse, the first thing they will do is scan the barcode on the product, instantly linking the items to your account. Amazon will know this because you will put the barcode number into the first tab on the product setup page here in Seller Central

Ok, so where do you get a bar code?

For the purposes of this initial exercise, where you're only working with your first handful of products, I am going to teach you the cheap and technically *incorrect* way.

Simply go to www.barcodesmania.com. Here you can buy a barcode for about $5. You get a unique barcode number, as well as the actual bar code itself. It takes 2 minutes.

Enter the barcode number into the first tab in Seller Central, and print as many barcodes as you need onto stickers you can buy from your local Staples or other office stationery outlet. Then place one barcode sticker onto each product.

That's it.

In all, bar coding should only cost you a few dollars and a trip to your local Staples.

So why is this way "technically" wrong and what is the *right* way?

Not long ago, Amazon distributed an email saying you had to use barcodes purchased from an organization called "GS1". GS1 is the governing body issuing barcodes for products world-wide. When you buy a barcode from GS1, your name (or your company name) is registered as the original and official owner of that barcode. The problem is the cost is over $100 to buy a single barcode and a lot more messing around.

When you buy from a site like www.barcodesmania.com, you are essentially buying a second-hand barcode, meaning Bar Codes Mania (or someone else) purchased the barcode from GS1 at some time in the past and if you (or anyone) search the GS1 barcode register, the original owner of that code comes up and not you.

Sites like Bar Codes Mania buy barcodes in bulk and resell them at a profit.

What I have prescribed here is the cheap and fast way to get started for the purposes of learning the process, rather than for the purposes of building a long-term business.

Hopefully that makes sense.

Let's move on to the last two steps.

STEP #5

This next step is to activate "FBA" (Fulfillment By Amazon), so that Amazon will warehouse your inventory and send out your orders. This really is essential and it's also where you'll learn a ton about how Amazon's FBA service actually works.

If you *don't* do this step, *you* will have to send out the product yourself when a sale happens. This means you're missing out on global expansion opportunities and a lifestyle business!

So to turn on FBA, all you have to do is the following:

From the main page of Seller Central, go to "Manage Inventory"

You will then see your product/s listed. What you need to do is select the product you want fulfilled by Amazon (by clicking the check box next to it) and hit the "edit" button on the right hand end of that product listing. Then select "Change to Fulfilled by Amazon".

That's it, you are now an Amazon FBA customer, and Amazon will now accept inventory you have sent into their warehouses.

How cool is that!

Let's go to the last step. You're almost there!

STEP #6

The final step is to actually send in your inventory. To do this, you need to create what's called a "shipping plan". This part is confusing the first time you do it, but once you've done it a few times, it becomes very easy as well.

The objective of this process is to tell Amazon exactly *what* you're sending, and *how* you're sending it to them. Amazon will then provide you with shipping labels to be attached to the cartons, and/or pallets you send the items in.

With your tiny shipment of AliExpress products, you'll do this labeling yourself by simply printing off the labels you receive from Amazon when you create the shipping plan. On future orders you make, you will email these labels to your suppliers in China (they're PDF files), and *they* will apply them to your goods and ship them directly to Amazon for you.

Quite often, Amazon will request you split your inventory up and send it to several different fulfillment centers in order for your products to be closer to the largest population centers they sell to.

For example, if you're sending in 100 cartons of golf balls, they might ask you to send 35 cartons to a Californian fulfillment center, 25 cartons to one of their Texas fulfillment centers, and then 40 cartons to one of their New York fulfillment centers. By doing this, they have your product close to consumers in the Western, Central, and Eastern parts of the country.

So here are the basics of how to create a shipping plan.

From the home page of Seller Central, click on "Inventory" and then "Manage FBA Inventory". You will find yourself at a page listing all of your products.

What you need to do is select the products you want to send in by checking the box next to each, and then select "Send Replenish Inventory". Once you do so, Amazon will guide you through the process of creating shipping labels for those products.

From this point, it's a case of following the steps. If you need help, you can either use Amazon's seller support, or you can get my course in which I teach all of this (and much more) via step-by-step recorded videos, webinars, and our global private Facebook group.

To learn more, visit www.reliable.education.

Ok, so now you know:

- How to buy some inventory quickly and cheaply
- How to open a Seller Central account
- How to create a SKU
- How to create a barcode
- How to create a listing in Seller Central
- How to convert the listing to FBA (Fulfilled By Amazon)
- How to create shipping labels so that you can send your inventory to Amazon

Wow! What a lot of learning in just a few pages!

Aren't books just the best?

Now that we have covered the boring technical stuff, let's get into the "meat and potatoes" of which kinds of products you should be looking for once you're ready to get serious about building a long-term portfolio of Amazon houses and hotels.

There's really four ways to approach finding products. You can do one or all of these, it's up to you. So let's take a look at these four ways:

1. Sit at home in your underpants, surfing the internet for product ideas.

2. Put your pants on and start hunting around all kinds of stores in your local area for ideas. Go to big box retailers like Walmart, as well as to specialist stores like surfing shops, camping stores, army supplies outlets, motorbike stores, and electronics retailers.

3. Join a trusted mastermind consisting of other people who want to start Amazon businesses and brainstorm together.

4. Go to a trade fair. Yes, going to China is great, but depending on what you want to sell, there may be great trade fairs locally ranging from "Sexpos" to Electronics and Car shows. All you're looking for at this stage are *ideas*.

No matter which path you choose, it's always helpful to have a checklist of things you're looking for. Checklists make it easy to quickly qualify or disqualify certain ideas without letting emotions get involved.

One thing you should know is checklists are a personal thing. There is no wrong or right way. Some things will be on your checklist for moral reasons, while others may be a function of your financial capacity.

For example, you might be morally against selling sex toys, but you have a larger appetite for risk than someone who has very little savings.

Your list will look different to others' and that's OK.

Just on that sex toys thing, you should know that some categories require approval from Amazon before you can sell in them, and others are closed to advertising even if you are approved. Sex toys happen to require approval in order to sell them *and* you can't advertise many products in this category, even if you are approved. This may be a total deal breaker! How else are you going to let people know about your beautifully boxed and branded vibrator if you cannot buy ads on Amazon? They're not the easiest thing to get reviews on either.

Just saying!

Here's a list of categories requiring approval at the time of writing this book.

- Automotive & Power sports
- Beauty, Clothing & Accessories
- Collectible Books
- Collectible Coins
- Entertainment Collectibles
- Fine Art
- Gift Cards
- Grocery & Gourmet Foods
- Health & Personal Care

- Independent Design
- Jewelry
- Luggage & Travel Accessories
- Major Appliances
- Services
- Sexual Wellness
- Shoes, Handbags & Sunglasses
- Sports Collectibles
- Textbook Rentals
- Textbook Rentals category.
- Video, DVD, & Blu-ray
- Watches
- Wine

This doesn't mean you cannot sell in these categories, it just means you will require approval from Amazon.

What is required to sell in these categories varies from one category to another, but here is an example of what's required to sell in "Luggage & Travel Accessories" (text taken straight from Amazon). The stars ************ indicate the start and end of Amazon's wording.

Amazon limits the addition of new sellers in the Luggage & Travel Accessories category to ensure customers are able to buy with confidence from all sellers on Amazon.

The requirements for selling in Luggage & Travel Accessories reflect buyer concern for product quality, product branding, and consumer safety.

Sellers must meet the requirements listed below to apply to sell products in the Luggage & Travel Accessories category. Please take the time to read this list of requirements and consult our help pages if you have questions about specific policies.

Once you have reviewed the category requirements, you can apply for approval by clicking the Request Approval button at the bottom of the page.

Meeting these requirements does not guarantee that Amazon will approve sellers for selling in Luggage & Travel Accessories. Please note that Amazon may remove approval to sell in the category for failure to meet these requirements.

Product-specific requirements

- All Luggage & Travel Accessories products must be new with tags.
- We do not allow the sale of irregular, seconds, or used products.
- All products must meet North American product safety standards.

- All products must be authentic. Sellers may not sell counterfeit or knock-off products.

- All products must be sold as listed. Buyers must be able to complete all aspects of ordering and purchasing a product using only the Amazon website. We do not allow custom listings that would require buyers to communicate with sellers before or after the purchase in order to receive the product they want.

- Sellers must review Seller Central listing guidelines and follow Amazon listing standards for any product sold on Amazon.

- When requesting approval to sell in Luggage & Travel Accessories, sellers must submit a complete list of brands that they plan to list. For private label products, sellers must indicate whether or not they are the sole manufacturer of the private label brand.

- All major brands must have UPCs. Amazon may grant partial UPC exemptions for private label brands. For information on the Luggage & Travel Accessories UPC exemption policy and a downloadable list of the brands that require UPCs, please see the Luggage & Travel Accessories UPC Exemptions

- All listing data and images must be suitable for all ages and appropriate for our global community. Listing data and images may not depict or contain nudity or pornographic, obscene or offensive items.

Product-specific Listing requirements

Sellers must appropriately and accurately classify their products.

Sellers must submit product titles, bullets, and product descriptions that are clearly written and assist the customer in understanding the product.

Listing variations

Items that come in multiple sizes or colors must be set up in a variation relationship. If you are only carrying one size, you are still required to create a variation with a parent SKU and list the buyable item on a child SKU.

Image Requirements

Your product images must meet certain technical and style requirements. Failure to meet the requirements can result in the suspension of your seller account.

Please ensure your images meet our requirements. Each image must be:

- On a pure white background.
- A color photograph.
- Devoid of any borders, watermarks, text, or other decoration.
- At least 1,001 pixels on its longest side. This allows customers to zoom in on your product image, which provides a detailed look and may reduce returns and negative feedback.

- Showing the entire product, occupying at least 85% of the image area.

- Of the product alone - no accessories, models, or mannequins.

- Showing a single view of the product - no alternate angles or close-ups.

For bundled products, it is not necessary to show the entire lot. A single image of the product is appropriate. For the main image for child products, ensure that the image represents the actual child product being listed. For example, if you are listing different colors of the same product, provide a child image that represents the color of the specific variation.

Prohibited

Do not use or include the following in product images:

- Product packaging or temporary tags not intended to be left on the product after purchase.

- Second hand or slightly used products.

- Borders, watermarks, text, or other decorations.

- Sketches or drawings of the product. Use photographic images only.

- Colored backgrounds or lifestyle pictures.

- Mannequins.

- Other products, items, or accessories that are not part of the product listing. Only include exactly what the customer is buying.

- Image placeholders (for example, temporary images or "no image available" text).

- Multiple products.

- Graphs of product ratings.

- Promotional text such as "sale" or "free ship" (use Promotions instead).

Although this is a fair bit of writing, nothing is particularly prohibitive if you're making your own line of travel goods. It just requires a little creativity and persistence - so don't let this put you off too much.

So what exactly does my product wish list contain?

Here it is:

1. The microclimate must have enough volume in it to support me generating at least $3,000/month in gross sales. This will have to come from the section of travelers my product will target. In the next chapter, I'll show you how we establish demand *before* we go into a microclimate.

2. Design must be important to my target traveler.

3. I must be selling into a microclimate where my branding skills will make me stand out. If there's already a bunch of great Peacocks on page #1 then I am not going to make the impact that I want, especially if they have tons of reviews and I don't.

4. I must believe that if I invest in branding, enough travelers will pay a premium to buy my product. Is it that type of product?

5. Is there an opportunity to compete with only one or two Peacocks and beat them on price? If yes, I'm interested, especially if I can see that those one or two Peacocks are making money.

6. Can I create photos to make my listing the #1 or #2 best listing on page #1, if assessed on photo quality alone?

7. Item should have few or no moving parts.

8. Item should not be too complex and made up of many pieces.

9. Item should not be seasonal (like pool chairs).

10. Item should not be fashion based - another form of seasonality.

11. Item should not be deep in Lion Territory. Think consumables like toothpaste, paper towels, and water.

12. Item should not be in microclimates crowded with Monkeys. Think most pills and potions.

13. Item should not expire (like food).

14. Where possible, the experience of the item should not be subjective. For example, the taste of a coffee or a protein powder is very subjective to the particular user. This can lead to bad reviews even though their opinion is highly subjective.

15. The reviews that the product could receive should not be dependent on the customer getting a particular

result. For example, weight loss creams. There are many variables out of your control that could affect the customer's opinion of the product - an opinion they will air in public in their reviews.

16. Item should not be fragile.

17. When I search for the product on Amazon, and tabulate the number of reviews that each product on page #1 has, no more than three of the 20 results should have more than 400 reviews. The rest should be under 100 reviews.

18. The product is viable in multiple Amazon markets.

19. The product doesn't need an instruction manual to be able to use it.

20. Can I sell this for 5X what the supplier is asking for it? So if I am paying $5 for it in China, can I get $25 for it on Amazon?

21. Am I morally OK with selling this product?

22. The sales rank of the top three products for the main keywords you use to find the product is under 10,000 for the category. I'll explain this shortly.

23. Have a retail price between $40 and $300.

This is my list, and mine will be different to yours. My list is much shorter than that of most people starting Amazon businesses.

For example, many people have:

- The product must weigh less than a pound
- The product must be less than 8 x 8 x 8 inches

- Must retail for between $15-$60

- The top three keywords must have a combined monthly search volume of more than 100,000 searches a month. You can use a piece of software called Merchant Words to discover this.

These are all great things to have in your list as well, but they may not be deal killers for everyone, especially those with a little more money.

Bigger, heavier and more expensive items are often less attractive to most people because they are more expensive to freight and require more capital. For these reasons, many beginners avoid them because they want things fast, easy, and at no risk. The challenge, of course, is there are more people looking for "fast, easy and low risk", than looking for "slower, bulkier and more expensive".

People with funds, risk appetite, and patience for the latter will naturally have fewer competitors when they get to market. That's the upside of the risk.

I personally like things more difficult to get into because it means I have somewhat of a moat around my castle once it's built.

However, I am not the most successful Amazon Seller I know by a long shot! It depends on how you measure success. I have many friends and some students making tons more money than me. Many of them are in pills and potions or cheap, high-demand products costing $20/unit. They are absolutely killing it and they're happy.

In 2015, I was interviewed by WebRetailer.com. When the story ran, I was delighted to see the headline, "Meet the lazy Amazon Seller." Like me, Web Retailer thought it was great that I was running a multi-national Amazon business while working about 20 minutes a day. To me, time is one of my biggest goals rather than just money. Everyone's definition of success is different.

I have rules based on knowing who I am, and how I want my life to be.

That last sentence may well be one of the most valuable pieces of advice I can give you. I believe businesses should *support* your life, rather than *define* it.

Too many entrepreneurs rush off into the world of business with a singular directive. Make money! That's all they want to do. It's a bit like a teenage boy wading into his sexuality for the first time. At first, the interest of any female at all is both welcomed and desired. In time, though, we get better at defining the less obvious variables that determine long-term compatibility.

Building an Amazon business is much the same.

There is no fast way to making millions on Amazon. It simply doesn't exist. A good checklist will make the journey a lot more bearable.

Amazon is one of those paradoxical business models whereby the more successful you become, the less money you seem to have. The reason being every time a successful seller turns around, they've sold out their inventory and they need more. More of the same stuff and more new lines to keep growing!

In his fantastic memoir "Shoe Dog", Phil Knight, the founder of Nike, stated he was basically flat broke right up to the day Nike went public. Nike had $269M in annual sales at that time, yet Phil hadn't lived a day where he wasn't fending off banks and finding new ones to give him more money to fund the enormous appetite for his Nike products.

Just like Nike, your profits will be driven by the same fundamentals outlined in my Velocity Retailing Formula.

Capital x Return x Rotations = Income

Without capital for inventory, you have no business!

So you either start out with capital, or you compound what you have to build it. Either way, success takes time. Unfortunately, this is not a popular message these days.

For this reason, I believe you need to think carefully about the kind of business you want to build and your income stability once your houses and hotels on the Amazon monopoly board are established.

My product checklist dictated that I move into fairly unique microclimates where not many new people move each day and where the cost of getting started is a little higher.

My advice to you is to put great thought into your approach to your business and be super honest about who you are.

Some of my friends are Monkeys to the core. They can take an average product and make $100,000/month on Amazon inside

of 3 months. Sooner or later the product crashes, but no problem, they've already got three more on the go!

I'll probably never earn what a hard-core Monkey earns, but I'm
part Peacock, part Monkey, and part Sloth. Yep, I'll own it! It's
who I am.

It's this tapestry of contrast which makes up this wonderful
thing we call "the jungle". Your job is to identify your strengths
and play to them. That's how it's always worked and why we
have so many wondrous creatures today.

To finish off this chapter, let's talk about some of the places you
can go to find awesome products to sell.

As you've learned earlier in the book, going to China or shopping at your local malls and specialty stores is a great place to
start. Let's leave that aside and talk about where you can go
online to find cool products. This way you can stay in your underpants and build a business at the same time!

The first place to start is obviously Amazon itself. Start in kids
toys and click over to automotive accessories. From there,
you might jump into camping goods or jumping castles. Just
browse and tumble.

Another great place is alibaba.com - the wholesale site I taught
you about earlier. Alibaba is different to Amazon because it
serves a truly global audience. You'll find stuff on there that
you've never seen in your home country.

WHAT SHOULD I SELL ON AMAZON?

When I start getting a few ideas about general products I'm interested in, I also like to go to Pinterest and do a search, usually, preceded by any of the following words:

- weird

- awesome

- amazing

- incredible

- designer

Let's say you are interested in tents - go to Pinterest (and maybe Google images), and type in, "weird tents", "awesome tents", "amazing tents", "incredible tents", and "designer tents". You'll be amazed at what shows up. You can then find some visually outstanding tents and try to find the supplier, or find a supplier to produce something similar.

When online, it's all about being creative and looking for what's different.

I would also monitor kickstarter.com, TouchOfModern.com, and other sites like these that curate products with outstanding design.

Get creative and have fun!

CHAPTER 7

★★★★★

RESEARCH FOR
SUCCESS AND **PROFIT**

A wonderful thing about Amazon these days is the fantastic software tools made by third party developers. These help you research product opportunities, identify keywords to put in your listing meta-data, and automate some key aspects of running your business.

I'm going to get into some of these tools in this chapter, but before I do, let's talk about the two levels of information that make up a product listing on Amazon.

In the previous chapter, I took you backstage and showed you the inside of Seller Central. Remember the seven tabs of information you have to complete in order to list a product on Amazon? Some of the content you added will show up on your public product listing on Amazon, but not all of it will. Keywords are just for Amazon's algorithm to know what it is you are selling. They won't all show on the public page your customers see.

The second level of information is the content anyone can see when looking at your listing on Amazon. If you know what you're looking at, you can learn an awful lot about a product and microclimate just by knowing what to look for on the public listing page.

Let's begin with photos. Remember I said photos had to be amazing? In a 10 minute period you can look at a bunch of competitors' photos in the microclimate you're interested in and quickly determine how many Peacocks, Monkeys, and Sloths you're dealing with.

A dead-giveaway you're in Sloth territory is when you notice the seller hasn't had professional photos taken or even used up all the photo slots available to them. You'll be amazed how often you see sellers have only added one photo!

In many cases, for big companies, Amazon is only one distribution channel for their products. They probably have a junior employee they're paying $15/hour to responsible for pushing all of their products onto Amazon. You can eat those guys for breakfast!

Next, take a look at the results popping up on page #1 for the main keyword (or words) you think people will type into Amazon to find the product you're interested in selling.

Next, take a pen and paper and write down how many reviews each of the top 20 results have.

Just like this:

Position #1=	234 Reviews
Position #2 =	141 Reviews
Position #3 =	101 Reviews
Position #4 =	23 Reviews
Position #5 =	44 Reviews
Position #6 =	18 Reviews
Position #7 =	121 Reviews
Position #8 =	22 Reviews

Position #9 =   55 Reviews

Position #10 =   12 Reviews

Position #11 =   99 Reviews

Position #12 =   14 Reviews

Position #13 =   77 Reviews

Position #14 =   6 Reviews

Position #15 =   16 Reviews

Position #16 =   5 Reviews

Position #17 =   32 Reviews

Position #18 =   12 Reviews

Position #19 =   8 Reviews

Position #20 =   113 Reviews

This data actually tells you a lot. In an instant, I can tell there are probably no Lions roaming in this area of the jungle. I'll tell you why in a moment.

What I like to do is ignore the top three results (those with the highest number of reviews), and then work out the average of the remaining 17 products on page #1. In this case, the top three products on this basis are position #1 (234 reviews), position #2 (141 reviews), and position #7 (121 reviews).

If you add up the number of reviews the remaining 17 listings have you'll get the number 657. Now divide 657 by 17 (the number of listings you added), and you'll notice the average number of reviews is 38.

That's a great number because it means if you make a great product that actually sells, and follow up with your customers, then there's a very good chance you will get enough reviews to look the part on page #1 for your product.

Remember I mentioned I could tell there are probably no Lions roaming these fields even before I picked up the calculator? Here's how I knew:

Lions only hunt in microclimates where there's a LOT of product being sold. They're interested in batteries, toothpaste, diapers and deodorant. Products millions of people buy, and use over and over again.

Just by virtue of sheer numbers, the top products in microclimates like these everyday products have a lot more reviews, usually in high hundreds or even thousands. The top 10 results of a product in Lion territory might look more like this:

Position #1 =	2,234 Reviews
Position #2 =	1,418 Reviews
Position #3 =	897 Reviews
Position #4 =	1,766 Reviews
Position #5 =	698 Reviews
Position #6 =	552 Reviews
Position #7 =	3,156 Reviews
Position #8 =	2,432 Reviews
Position #9 =	299 Reviews
Position #10 =	98 Reviews

These are big microclimates where Lions and/or Monkeys abound.

If you want to break into these microclimates, you're going to need either a genuinely unique product to stand out the moment you see it, or a similar looking product to the other results on page #1 at a <u>much</u> better price.

If you have a product with either of those criteria (or both) you can run ads for your product from day-1 and it will probably sell well even though you have far less reviews.

Theoretically, once you start selling a lot, even if it's your advertising driving the volume, you should soon see your product climbing the organic results as well, because Amazon loves to show products that *sell* well. Why? Because Amazon gets paid every time a transaction happens, so naturally they want to show the best selling products first.

Make sense?

For now, understand that by purely looking at the *number* of reviews the average product on page #1 has in the microclimate you're interested in you get a pretty quick feel for how much traffic goes through that area of the jungle and what kind of animals you're likely to find there.

Generally speaking, high numbers means lots of sales. Low numbers means lower sales. That being said, if you scrutinize, you'll still find plenty of microclimates where there are very few Monkeys or Peacocks and no Lions at all. Incredibly, there are still areas of the jungle where Sloths are lazily and quietly making a fortune.

Let me give you an example...

In 2014, I formed a Mastermind of five friends, all of whom wanted to start Amazon businesses. Every month we'd buy a bottle of wine and meet at either my office in Hollywood, or at one of the guy's houses high in the Hollywood Hills overlooking LA. Despite the fact we were all friends, and despite the fact most of us were having a drink, we actually had a fairly solid structure to keep these meetings focused and on track.

To start off the night, we each reminded the group of the action items we publicly committed to doing in the prior meeting a month before. We then had to report on each item and what we *actually* did. This kept us accountable, because if you missed your goals, the group universally derided you as a loser (in a very loving way).

Once the reports were done, it was one person's turn in the hot seat. That person had the full attention and focus of the group. They could talk about whatever they wanted with regards to advancing their Amazon goals. One of the first to take that hot seat was my good friend Jon who, at the time, was a senior account manager at one of LA's most well regarded advertising agencies.

Jon was doing well at his job, but like most corporate jobs, he had very little time and almost no location freedom. He had to work in the office, or at least in LA, most of the time. He couldn't travel, set his own hours, or work harder to massively increase his income. Jon needed to become an entrepreneur.

On this particular evening, Jon had prepared a detailed set of tables that analyzed the strengths and weaknesses of about 20 products that he was interested in starting out with. As we looked over his research, one of these stuck out like crazy.

The top selling item in that microclimate was doing about $30,000/month in sales (I'll explain later in this chapter how to figure that out), but the seller only had 38 reviews, and the rest of the page #1 listings had less. Not only that, the top product had average photos, the reviews weren't great, and headlines and sales copy were poor.

Jon had found the Holy Grail. A microclimate where Sloths were getting rich, and no Lions, Peacocks, or Monkeys in sight.

We all voted and Jon decided to go for it.

To cut a long story short, within 90 days, Jon was doing $50,000/month in sales off that one product, at about a 40% profit margin. Using his Peacock and Monkey skills, he created a better product, he branded it better, and then he sold it at the same price as the Sloths. In short order, he took all the business and he's never looked back.

Sometimes you only need to stand out in one area to take decent market share from other inhabitants of any microclimate. While Jon found a Unicorn, where the Sloths were doing *everything* poorly, others have done well because the other sellers are Peacocks with awful Monkey skills. In other words, their competitors have great products but no idea what they're doing with keywords so rarely get found.

Other times there are listings where the sellers are Sloths when it comes to asking their customers for reviews (a Monkey skill).

They simply don't send any emails after the sale, something easy to setup and automate with software I'm going to tell you about in this chapter. This is only something you find out if you do what I said earlier in this book and buy your competitors' products on Amazon.

There are all kinds of advantages to be had in the jungle. It's your job to train your eyes to see the gaps and fill them.

OK, we've talked about photos, reviews, and a little about email follow up. Now let's teach you about how else to spot the various animals selling in your microclimate of interest just by looking at their Amazon listing.

The next things I look at are headlines, bullet points, and descriptions. How well written are they? Do they contain lots of keywords? Do they *sell* the item or just *describe* it? Are they offering coupons or multi-purchase discounts in their product description (true Monkey behavior)?

Finally, I actually read the reviews of some of the top ranked items, especially the 1, 2 and 3-star reviews. It's in these reviews I discover a plethora of ways to make improvements to the product itself if I decide to go into that microclimate.

I also find tons of content for when it comes time for me to write my own product descriptions. Let me give you an example.

Let's say I am thinking of selling a Coffee Press.

If I read the reviews of the top ranked products and I see dozens of people are complaining about the *size* of the Presses on the market, then that's something I'll hunt for in my sourcing. When

I have a larger Press, and I'm writing my product description, I'll add a line that might say, "This Coffee Press is 400ml which is 150ml larger than most Coffee Presses on Amazon. This will give you 4 full cups as opposed to 2.5."

Reading the bad reviews, you might also learn your competitors' product has a cheap filter in the press, and as a result, coffee grains are leaking through the gauge and into the coffee. Very frustrating when you're hardly awake in the morning! You don't want a review from a pre-caffeinated American!

After spending a few hours touring your microclimate of interest, and carefully assessing how many Peacocks, Monkeys and Sloths there are, you start getting a sense of where the opportunities are and where not.

The last step in the process is to peruse what's called "The Best Seller Rank" or BSR. This metric shows beneath the product description on every Amazon page, indicating how popular a product is in relation to all other products in that category.

For example, if a cutting board has a BSR of 5,678 in the "Home & Kitchen" category, it is saying of all the products in "Home & Kitchen" (probably hundreds of thousands), this board is the 5,678th best selling item. It's a quick method of seeing the overall popularity of the item.

There are many Amazon experts out there, and we each have a different opinion about BSR. Some say you should only sell products in the top 1,000 of the main category in which they're listed. Others say the top 5,000 or 10,000.

Aside from me, though, I have met very few (none yet) saying the BSR is the *last* thing you would check.

So why do I consider it to be the last step?

Well, in some aspects, the other experts are right. Making sure there's demand for a product is very important, but demand and profit margin are very different things. As is demand and your ability to gain traction. BSR doesn't tell you these things. Real research does.

What tells you how likely you are to gain traction (and make money), is your ability to identify the other creatures living there and their relative competency as Amazon sellers. If you go into a really high selling microclimate, but you don't know how to identify a Lion from a Sloth, there's a very good chance that you'll be eaten alive!

The other reason I don't rate BSR as universally important, is that sometimes there's great money in more expensive items where overall volumes are lower. For example, I've had products with a BSR of over 50,000 in their category, but selling for nearly $200 a piece. This means I can sell ten times *less volume* than a $20 product and make the same money. My *volume* will never see me rank high on BSR, but I make a nice, low competition income there!

It's for these reasons I encourage my students and anyone reading my book to develop their *qualitative* research skills first, and then move into *quantitative* analysis second.

Ok, to close out this chapter, let's talk about the software tool I use to help me research product opportunities, monitor my reviews, automate my email follow up, and do a few other things besides.

It is software called ZonGuru. You will find it online at www.zonguru.com

In the interests of full disclosure, I am the founder of ZonGuru, and the CEO is my friend Jon, whom I mentioned earlier in this chapter. We built the software from scratch after learning exactly what sellers' need because we ourselves were in the marketplace every single day.

If you're totally new to Amazon, the first tool you'll most likely use is called Sales Spy. This tool allows you to track the sales of almost any product on Amazon. This is incredibly powerful and gives you a phenomenal insight into how much money you might make before you spend a dime. It was while using ZonGuru that Jon discovered the potential of his hit product discussed earlier.

The next most popular tool in ZonGuru is the Email Automator. This tool enables you to setup a series of emails to automatically go out to your customers after they buy from you on Amazon. This tool is incredibly helpful for a few reasons.

First, the one big downside of selling on Amazon is you don't get your customer's email addresses. This is because Amazon considers them *their* customer, not yours. So if you want to communicate with people who buy your products on Amazon, you have to login to Seller Central, find the customer, and type them a message.

It's not like normal ecommerce where the customer buys something on your website, you capture their email address, and email them whatever and whenever you want.

ZonGuru connects to your Seller Central account, and with the Email Automator tool, you can set up emails to go out automatically at intervals determined by you.

For example, you might program one email to go out immediately after a customer buys, just saying thank you and confirming their order. You might program another one to go out six days later, just checking in to confirm everything arrived OK and undamaged. Then you might program one final email, 20 days after, requesting a review.

By doing this, you achieve a bunch of really important things.

First, you are providing outstanding service. You will be amazed at how often we receive emails from customers saying that in all the years they've bought on Amazon, they've never heard anything from the actual seller of the product. This continues to blow our minds!

Second, by following up like this, you get ahead of any problems *before* they become a bad review. In these first two emails, you inform your customers that "If there's anything wrong with your product, in any way at all, please email me first. I will do my absolute best to fix the problem immediately."

I cannot tell you how many times this has saved us getting bad reviews! One of the best and worst things about the FBA and private label model is you don't touch or see your own products. They literally go from your manufacturer to your customer and you haven't seen or touched a thing.

The good part about this is massive leverage. The bad part is your customers are the first people to notice any problems. Sadly, if something messed up in the factory or broke during the shipping process anywhere between a remote factory in China and your customer's doorstep in America, then without the strong pre-emptive communication I'm describing here, the first you might know about an issue is when they've posted a 1-star review on Amazon.

ZonGuru and Email Automator is a fantastic tool for providing awesome service, getting ahead of problems, and finally, getting more reviews. Incredibly, most sellers on Amazon still don't use a tool like ZonGuru to send emails to people buying their products, or ask them politely for a review. In this regard, most sellers are still Sloths.

ZonGuru has a number of additional features, but check it out yourself.

You are now probably feeling better equipped to start observing the jungle and finding product opportunities.

I only wish I had this much training when I was starting out! To research and understand this stuff has taken years to learn and at great personal expense.

CHAPTER 8

★ ★ ★ ★ ★

GROW

You are, by now, probably becoming excited at the prospect of selling on Amazon. I know how I felt when I first got my head around it. I couldn't sleep!

It's hard to imagine you can launch a global brand without leaving whatever city you live in.

In a recent Facebook post made by one of our students who lives in the US, he exclaimed, "I woke up to a sale in Malta today. I don't even know where that is!"

This student had just listed his products in the UK and then activated his listings into 26 other European countries. Within 24 hours, he was making money from countries he didn't know the location of!

Imagine sitting in America, making money in Malta, and not having touched the item making you the money?

How the world has changed.

If you took my advice, and already have a small order of products on their way from China, then you're almost there!

With a little time and effort, you could be in business with one of the most valuable companies in the world, leveraging their assets, and making money 24/7 in multiple currencies as well.

So let me share with you my best tips for growing quickly.

First, if possible, test a small range of similar products (preferably from the same supplier), rather than allocating all of your money to one product. If you have $10,000 for example, try to get two or three different products going rather than just one. Or, if it makes sense for the product you are selling, order two or three colors instead of one. You never know what's going to sell.

In my friend Jon's case, his product comes in two colors. One color sells four times better than the other. There is a very good reason for this, but Jon didn't figure that reason out until *after* he tested both. In hindsight, it was obvious why one would do better than the other, but we often miss things when we are trying to figure it all out in advance.

Another example is my brother Ben. Ben has a range of "Amazon properties" on the Amazon Monopoly board. He bought five different styles of the same kind of product in his very first order. Just like Jon, Ben discovered a hotel in those five properties, but he honestly had no inkling in advance as to which one would be the best seller.

If you can go a little wider than a single product early in your Amazon business, it will serve you well.

There are other reasons for starting with a small range of similar products as well.

First, a lot of the time in getting from zero to making money on Amazon is spent waiting for and tweaking samples. If you're going to be waiting a week for one sample from a supplier, you may as well be waiting for three or four. It just saves time and allows you to launch with a larger footprint and a greater chance of finding a hotel.

Second, by having more than one product in your portfolio, Amazon will often show your other products in the "Frequently Bought Together" Recommendations section of your listing page. This is known as "the halo effect" and it results in more sales. It also gives the customer more confidence in you when you are offering a range of products rather than just one.

So now, let's talk about the one thing nobody seems to want to talk about in the world on other Amazon courses:

How to fund your inventory.

As you know, the first variable in the Velocity Retailing formula is capital. No capital = no income.

If you're in a strong financial position, then this part may not be relevant for you, but for everyone else, you need to know how much inventory is going to be required to reach your personal goals.

Let's say your *income* goal is $100,000 a year. How much *inventory* is that going to require?

Let's begin with the following basic assumptions:

1. You make 30% return every time you rotate your inventory
2. You can rotate that inventory 3 times a year

Thus, the Velocity Retail Formula currently looks like this:

Capital x 30% x 3 = Income

Now, what figure needs to be in the *capital* variable to allow the *income* to be $100,000 in the end?

Let's see what happens if we stick the figure of $100,000 in the capital part.

$100,000 Capital x 30% Return ($30,000) x 3 rotations

= _____ income

Did you do the math? If you did, you'd see that the income figure turns out to be $90,000.

We're pretty close!

Let's see what happens if we change the return variable to 35% return instead of 30%.

$100,000 capital x 35% return ($35,000) x 3 rotations

= _____ income.

OK. What is the income now?

If you do the math, you'll quickly see we're now at $105,000 income.

Do you see how that works?

Now you understand the basic math, the question becomes, "How do I get $100,000 capital if I only have $5,000 now?"

I recently interviewed one of my students from Vancouver, Canada. He is just 22 years old, and at the time of the interview, he was averaging around $60,000/month in sales on

Amazon after just 18 months on the platform. At the rate he is going, and with a bump from Christmas sales, he'll probably do around $1,000,000 in sales this year. What's interesting is that he started with just $1,500.

Once you get the hang of selling on Amazon, and you have your brand and products developed, you'll quickly learn the name of the game is keeping your inventory in stock. For every month you're out of stock, you are losing money.

Let me give you an example.

If a product makes $5,000/month in sales and it runs out of stock, you're losing $5,000 in revenue every month. If you haven't already ordered new inventory at the time you run out, and you're shipping by sea, you could easily be out of stock for four months while the manufacturer makes your new order and then ships it. Four months x $5,000/month in sales = $20,000 you've missed out on!

Now imagine you've got *several* products like that and they all run out at the same time! This happens all the time with larger sellers. In fact, for the first three years of my own Amazon business, I seemed to have an uncanny knack of running out of stock right before the holiday season in America, the absolute *worst* time of year to run out of stock. I have literally lost hundreds of thousands of dollars in sales as a result.

When you have a product (or range of products) selling well, the name of the game is simple. Don't run out of stock!

Not running out of stock is about inventory management and money. First, you have to keep a close eye on what your monthly sales volumes are for each product you sell, and then you have to do some basic planning to make sure you aren't caught short on your inventory levels. In order to plan properly, you need to know two things:

1. How long your current inventory will last.
2. How long it takes your supplier to make your product and ship it all the way to Amazon.

The rest is just logic.

Once you know how much you need, the second part of this is money. You need to be able to fund this investment into inventory.

After years of running service-based businesses where my *time* was my inventory, this really took some adjustment on my side. I also see people who've had jobs their whole lives struggle with the concept of investing money upfront to ensure an income later down the line. It's a total shift in mindset. The payoff though, is that your money goes to work and brings home the income, not you!

As I mentioned earlier in this book, a great book to pick up that really drives this mindset home is "Shoe Dog" - the memoir of Nike's founder, Phil Knight. Like most people I've spoken to about the book, I was shocked to find Mr. Knight was personally broke right up until he took Nike public in 1980. In that year, they did $269,000,000 in sales, but he still lived in the same house he'd always lived in because, until that point, every cent he had personally he kept investing back into inventory and growth. He is the ultimate marshmallow kid!

If you aren't in a position to fund your growth, and you don't want to wait for the effects of compounding to kick in, then you're probably going to have to fund your growth by borrowing from friends, family, banks, and perhaps even credit card companies.

The key thing to remember here is this kind of borrowing is what I call "good debt" (as opposed to bad debt), because unlike most things people borrow money for, an investment in inventory brings back the borrowed capital _AND_ it brings back a profit.

Let me give you a real example of how I accelerated my growth by borrowing $21,000.

After two years of selling on Amazon, I started getting emails from a division of Amazon called Amazon Lending. I actually hadn't heard of them before, but essentially, it's a division of Amazon that lends money to sellers they have pre-approved based on knowing their sales and how long it takes them to sell their inventory. It's an invitation-only program that cannot be proactively applied for. They reach out to you, not the other way around.

I had ignored them for months, but at the start of 2016, I found a product I wanted to launch, and Amazon Lending sent another email offering me money. I decided to take a small loan of $21,000 and pay it back in six equal payments over six months.

The interest rate was 15.9% annually, and the monthly payments were $3,664. There were no other fees.

So let's do the math.

They would lend me $21,000 immediately.

I would make six payments of $3,664 over six months to pay them back.

6 x $3,664 = $21,984

So in total, I would pay only $984 on top of the $21,000 I borrowed. How good is that?

I accepted their terms by clicking one box on an online form (without having to show any further financials), and they instantly credited my account with the $21,000.

For Amazon, this was a low risk loan because they had all the data on my seller account, and they already knew who I was.

What was really great is that the payments were made by simply deducting them from my fortnightly payments from Amazon. In other words, if I was due $30,000 for my sales for the last two weeks, they would send me $30,000 less my loan repayment. It was totally seamless!

That $21,000 enabled me to buy inventory that sold for five times that amount on Amazon.

5 x $21,000 = $105,000 in sales.

Of that, around 40% (or $40,000) was profit.

So in short, for the $984 in fees I paid Amazon, I got $40,000 back in profit *after* paying back the loan.

Amazing!

At 15.9% per year, this wasn't exactly cheap money in the context of loans, but when you consider I paid it back in six months, and then multiplied it substantially because of Amazon, the rate is almost irrelevant.

Please be aware that at the time I borrowed the money I had been selling on Amazon for a few years. I knew, with a fair amount of certainty, I'd get this money back safely. You should always only borrow what you feel comfortable with, but "good debt" can be a very powerful tool to grow your wealth.

The name of the game here is to start with what you have, prove you know what you're doing, and then getting the money shouldn't be difficult. Many people out there would love a better return than they're currently getting from the banks and stock markets. You just have to be able to prove your worth.

What's really great these days is the emergence of peer-to-peer lending platforms where you can literally have strangers lend you money in much the same way as Amazon privately financed me. Some of the big platforms are:

- www.lendingclub.com

- www.prosper.com

- www.fundingcircle.com

These are all US based but similar sites are popping up all over the world.

In Australia and New Zealand for example, there is a site called www.harmoney.com.au (Australia) and www.harmoney.co.nz (New Zealand). As I am writing this book, they've lent in excess of $400M to private borrowers without a bank in sight!

Google is your friend here. Just type in "crowd sourced loans <insert country>" or "peer to peer lending <insert country>".

I love these platforms because they take your loan directly to private investors while using other metrics than your credit score to approve or deny your loan. Some of them use AI algorithms and social media profiling as well. They are very sophisticated and super efficient.

The key to borrowing responsibly is to be aware that if it all goes pear-shaped, you can, in fact, repay the loan from other sources of cash flow. My advice is to be responsible and increase your borrowing in-step with your knowledge and experience.

My final word of advice around growing an Amazon business is to continue growing as a businessperson. Rarely does income outstrip competency. If you want to grow your *income* beyond where you are today, then *you* are going to have to grow beyond where you are today as well.

Keep reading books, attending seminars, and increasing your network of like-minded entrepreneurs. When things get tough it will be your personal growth and network of people that will get you through. If all of your friends have jobs, then you probably won't get the advice you need when things get tough. It's essential to expose yourself to other people who know, from first-hand experience, how tough building a business can be.

CHAPTER 9

★★★★★

AUTOMATE

In my opinion, a business is only a business when it makes money *without* the owner being there. If it requires your presence, then you are obligated to be there in the same way you're obligated to go to work in order to get your pay.

As your Amazon business grows, if you don't automate some things and hire others to help, you won't really have a business at all. You'll have an online customer support and wholesaling business requiring your ongoing attention.

Here are the main areas of an Amazon business requiring humans to be involved once you grow.

- Handling customer inquiries and issues
- Managing inventory and inbound shipments
- Maintaining your listings on Amazon, keywords, reviews, sales copy and photos
- Keeping an eye on your Amazon advertising campaigns
- Monitoring your microclimate and staying aware of what's happening in your little section of the jungle
- Researching new product ideas

These six things are a constant once you're established.

Let's begin with customer service first.

Mostly, my customer service issues arise out of my proactive approach to getting ahead of any issues before they become bad reviews by sending outbound emails after the customer buys. In every product box I send, there's a short note thanking the customer for buying my product and telling them how to reach us in the event anything is wrong, no matter how small.

This is the source of 90% of our customer service emails, but it's also why most of my products have a solid 5-star rating. We fix issues before they become negative reviews. One free product is always less expensive than a 1-star review which will stay with your product for life.

Before I get into how I've outsourced my customer support, let me share with you the actual emails I have running in ZonGuru to automate the outbound email process to all customers.

Email #1

Sent immediately after they order on Amazon.

Message subject: Thank you

Hello [[first-name]],

I just wanted to sincerely THANK YOU for your order with us. I am sure you are going to love this product!

I just wanted to let you know that Amazon has now shipped your order.

I'll reach out in a few days time just to make sure everything arrived as expected. If you have any questions at all, please don't hesitate to let us know by simply replying to this email.

It is our goal that you have an exceptional buying experience with us.

Kindly,
Your name
Your company name

Email #2

Sent six days following the customer order.

Message subject: Did everything arrive ok?

Hello [[first-name]],

I just wanted to make sure you received your product OK.

If you had any issues at all, please let me know right away.

We pride ourselves on our customers being delighted so please let me know if there were any issues. I'll do everything I can to make it right!

Have a wonderful day and thanks again for your business.

Kindly,
Your name
Your company name

Email #3

Sent 14 days after order.

Message subject: Good news

Hello [[first-name]],

The reason for this email is just to make sure that you were happy in every way with your purchase. It is the last email we will send :-)

If you were happy with your experience, it would be AMAZING if you could take two minutes and leave us a product review on Amazon. As a small business in a competitive market, these REALLY help us.

You can leave a review here:

[[product-review-link]]

If there were any problems at all, please let me know so we can attempt to make it right. We really value our customers and we respond to every single email.

I hope you're having a wonderful day and thanks again for being a customer!

Kindly,
Your name
Your company name

See how simple and unpretentious they are? I am not trying to come off as some big impersonal company. I want them to feel like they are dealing with a small business owner who really cares about their experience, because I do!

You'll be amazed at how effective these are in getting people to tell you about problems, share their gratitude, and write nice reviews for you.

What's awesome is that ZonGuru does all of this automatically. It takes about five minutes to set up and they work around the clock, building relationships and racking up reviews on autopilot.

As mentioned earlier, these do create *inbound* email traffic requiring response. It "has to be", because Amazon actually time how long you take to respond to every single email you get through their platform. If you don't respond within 24 hours, your seller rank gets affected.

At first, I didn't realize *every* email has to be acknowledged, even if it doesn't require a response. For example, some people write back and say, "Thank you, I got your product", and that's it. In a case like this, there is no need to write a response but you do need to acknowledge their email.

For this purpose, Amazon has a little button in their email program inside of seller central called "No Response Needed". By checking this, you are telling Amazon you've read the customer's email but it doesn't require an answer, and then you won't get dinged. So always click this button if you're not responding!

While at first this may seem like a drag, initiatives like this on Amazon's part make people love Amazon and spend more on their site with confidence. Amazon is forcing us all to be better business people. Customers benefit as a result.

I have a part time employee I found through www.upwork.com who handles all of these responses for me. I only get about 15 emails a day and he charges me about $100/week for the work he does. He is a New Zealand guy who speaks English as a first language. He is more expensive than had I hired a worker in one of the lower cost countries like the Philippines or India. Personally, I'd rather pay an extra $50/week and have an employee who understands the nuances of the English language. After all, money isn't my highest value at this point. Ease of doing business is. Remember how I encouraged you earlier to build a business around *your* values?

Whilst we are talking about employees, let's talk about how to get great ones. In the world of data, there is a widely used phrase stating "garbage in, garbage out." Normally, it's used to explain to business owners who are trying to collect data on their customers, that if they don't take the time to collect their customer's information properly, then the value of information a database software can give out is limited. Garbage in, garbage out.

When it comes to your employees, the same is also true. If you don't put time and training *into* employees, then it's illogical to expect excellence *out* of them.

In my companies, we hire and fire based on a pre-defined set of values. By having these values stated up front, it is really clear to the potential hire who we are as a company and whether or not they are a fit for how we do business. This is actually incredibly rare and incredibly powerful in business.

To get to a set of values for your business, it doesn't have to be some convoluted corporate exercise where you sit around in a circle holding hands and singing Kumbaya. Instead, just create what I call an "Always Never List". It's super simple.

On one side of the paper, write down 4-6 things you always do at your company. It can look like this:

At ACME Amazon Business, we <u>always</u>:

- Treat our customers with the highest respect and assume their problems are very real for them.
- Seek to "wow" our customers.
- Replace broken items without question.
- Remember how blessed we are to have a job and not be among the world's poorest who are begging for money or food.

Now, on the other side, you write your "never list". It might look like this:

At ACME Amazon Business, we <u>never</u>:

- Try to prove we are right and the customer is wrong.
- Speak about problems we have with co-workers without them being present.

- Act or speak in a way that could cause racist, sexist, sexual or religious offence. We believe all people are free to love whom they choose, worship whom they choose, and be who they really are, without fear of ridicule, hate, or slander.

- Bring a problem to a co-worker or manager without having found at least two possible solutions for that problem.

That's it. You now have your company's "starter values" and you can work on them over time.

I know this might seem simple, but this kind of simple detail ties into whom you are as a company in the same way the windows being polished at the Rolex store says something about how Rolex does business. Winners respect standards and want to work with other winners who have standards and express them as well.

The greatest thing about having clear and documented values is it creates a non-personal way of hiring and firing people. You are now less swayed by your personal biases, and more focused on how you want your company to show up in the world. If someone is constantly bitching about other employees, the firing conversation you have becomes really easy.

"Hey Sarah, you were just bitching about Sally and Sally wasn't there. How do you think your action aligns with our values?"

Instead of you feeling all messed up about having to fire Sarah if she doesn't stop doing it, it's a case of Sarah firing herself and you're just filling out the paperwork!

Make sense?

You might think all of this is overkill if you're hiring one offshore contractor, but believe me, it makes a huge difference. Humans crave positive structure and respect those giving it in a respectful way.

Once you have your values written down, if you really want to be free, you have to put *great* training into your team. Great training is what enables you to be wherever you want, whenever you want, without having to check your email every five minutes and worrying whether everything is falling to pieces.

Of all the tools I've used to train others how to run my digital businesses, "screen capture software" is by far the most important. Screen capture software records your computer screen while you narrate, so you can literally *show* your employee how the task is done while you talk to them at each step. More importantly, you can create the video whenever you want, and they can watch it whenever they want.

It's not only great for that employee, but once you have it, your video can be used to train every employee as your company scales or in the event your current employee leaves or keeps breaking your values.

I have a Mac and I use a piece of software called "Screen Flow" which is made by Telestream. I am pretty sure it is sold for PC as well.

I use this for everything, from teaching my financial controller how to pay people using our Internet banking, to how our customer service people are to send out a replacement products from Amazon's warehouse.

Basically, every time you find yourself doing a task you want someone else to do (which should be almost everything), get into the habit of recording yourself doing it on your computer and turn it into a little video. Within a few months' time, you'll have a training library of videos you can use to outsource the "doing" aspect of your business so that you can hang out at the beach.

Ok, so let's revisit the list of tasks established Amazon businesses create:

1. Handling customer inquiries and issues

2. Managing inventory and inbound shipments

3. Maintaining your listings on Amazon, keywords, reviews, sales copy and photos

4. Keeping an eye on your Amazon advertising campaigns

5. Monitoring your microclimate and staying aware of what's happening in your little section of the jungle

6. Researching new product ideas

We've ticked off #1, but what about the rest? How long does all that take?

In reality, only #1 is something requiring everyday attention and this is the first piece you should outsource as you scale. It's very process driven and relatively easy to pass off.

Task #2, managing inventory and inbound shipments, is only something you do a few times a year, and not something I will go into detail about in this book. This kind of training is available in my full online training program.

You can learn more about my training by visiting www.reliable. education

Remember, to set up a shipment in Seller Central only takes about 10-20 minutes (once you know what you're doing), and managing the inbound shipment process is usually handled by your freight forwarder. Again, I won't go into freight forwarding in this book, but I do cover it extensively in my online course.

Depending on which microclimate you're in, and where you sit in the niche, tasks #3, #4 and #5 may be tasks you do once a month, and they shouldn't take more than half a day. The reason I say, "depending on your microclimate and where you sit", is because if you're in something super competitive, and if you're sitting at the top of that niche, you may have to monitor this stuff daily. The other monkeys that live in that microclimate are going to be very active, and there will be new monkeys arriving daily.

Task #6, researching new products, is something you should be doing (at least passively), all the time. My friends tease me frequently because when I go to a shopping mall, I'll wander off to the Homeware stores and start chatting with middle age ladies who usually work there about which cheese platters and salad bowls are selling best, and which of the products in the store they like the best. I have become quite the expert when it comes to the latest designs in bed linen, kitchen tools, frying pans, and teapots.

The point of all of this is to have fun, express your creativity, and leverage yourself out of the tasks you don't enjoy. Business shouldn't be a drag and it's not all about money. After all, money, without the time to spend it, has no value, so be sure to put *time* on your list of things a business must produce.

CHAPTER 10

★ ★ ★ ★ ★

SELLING YOUR
AMAZON BUSINESS

Something I am big believer in, especially for first time entre-preneurs, is building and selling a company. There are many reasons for my way of thinking, but none is greater than learn-ing what it really takes to build something someone else is will-ing to pay you for. The focus and financial discipline required to achieve this goal will make you a better businessperson for life.

The other significant reason for building and selling a company is that even if the business makes only a few hundred thousand dollars profit a year, the value of the business, together with the value of its inventory on the day of sale, will enable most people to pay off their mortgage or buy a house. In so doing, they free themselves of the most significant debt they'll ever have - the home they live in.

Many financial experts will tell you that paying off your own home is a terrible financial decision and you could use the money to buy more investment properties (which mathemati-cally they're right about). In my opinion, however, there is something much more valuable that is unleashed when you no longer feel the pressure of debt or the need to work every single day to pay the banks.

For me, not having debt has had a profound impact on the way I think and the way I feel about life. You cannot put a price on those things. I also believe I make better decisions in life and business as I'm not under duress from the banks.

It's a bit like the day your profit from your side-business is enough to pay your rent or mortgage every month, and you're still earning what you always were at your job as well. That day is really special, and your life changes.

I have, so far, sold one of my companies through a private sale and taken another one onto the stock exchange. Both of these experiences taught me a great deal and both had life-changing consequences. What I can tell you for sure is, more than the money, it's who you become through the process that proves the real reward.

Not everyone shares the goal of owning their own home, and maybe cash flow really is your goal (rather than a big check). I get that. But let me offer a few observations that may make you consider the idea of selling your business once it's built.

First, what I've noticed about most people who earn more money is they increase their spending right along with it. They go from driving a basic car to driving a fancy car. They go from eating out occasionally, to eating out all the time. Holidays increase, personal trainers appear, and their quality of life goes up.

Their increased lease payments, mortgages, and rising tax bills eat away the salary increase and they never really see a substantial increase in their net worth.

They're going nowhere in more comfort.

You probably don't have to look far to see someone similar, perhaps not even beyond yourself. It's totally normal because very few of us don't want something better than we already have. Even fewer have the discipline of not having it when we actually *can* afford the payments!

When you sell a business, particularly one like Amazon where your cash flow has been reinvested for several years, you suddenly realize the wealth creation benefit *in one check* rather than drip-fed to you over years. This realization dynamic is profound.

Because you had nothing for so long, and then get it all at once, the *way* you view the money is very different. This is especially true when coupled with the fact you have just sold your income stream. You now have the proper appreciation for the money and you're much more likely to keep it!

The other thing most accountants and financial planners don't factor into things when giving advice to entrepreneurs is their ability to build another business - often very quickly.

So my message here is simple. Whilst it is possible to earn more, live modestly, and invest the difference, most don't do it and those that do, have to do it for a while before they get somewhere.

An entrepreneur, on the other hand, can work hard for three to five years and sell out for upwards of a million dollars then do it again in less time. Do you know many employees who have accumulated this kind of money in three to five years of saving and investing?

Aside from getting life changing checks, by selling your business you are de-risking your wealth creation. *Realizing* profit, opposed to paper profit, is sometimes a very different thing.

When I was still involved with the company I took public, I lost about $12,000,000 in "paper-wealth" in three months when the stock market crashed in 2008. Oh how I wished I'd converted some of my shares into cash just before that happened!

Herein is my next point about selling. There are very few businesses in the world that really are recession-proof, disruptor-proof, or totally without risk. *Everything* in business is risky! Even on Amazon, you never know how the microclimate you're in might change, or who might move into your territory tomorrow.

Things change, but when your chips are off the table, it doesn't matter. In fact, if things do turn bad, and you have cash, this is the time to invest and make your next fortune!

As I mentioned above, I lost a ton of paper money in 2008 and ended up working for free for nearly two years whilst selling every asset I had to save the company. It set me back years. One thing I did which really helped was investing the little spare cash I had into some blue-chip stocks that also got seriously hammered in the downturn. The stock I bought most of was trading at $15/share just before the crash. I bought it for 83c and sold it for $6 just six months later. That was only possible because I had some *actual* cash.

So what does it take to sell a business, and are Amazon businesses attractive?

Let me start with the value of Amazon businesses and their appeal in the marketplace. First, Amazon businesses require almost no staff. Anyone experienced in running a business know employees are not only the most expensive part of running a business, they are easily the most painful part to deal with, and carry risk the most risk. An employee-free business is a dream-business.

Next, there are no leases. Aside from the fact that leases are expensive, they don't go away even if your business fails. They can be a huge sticking point when you go to sell.

When you deal with a business broker, they'll tell you the #1 most painful aspect of selling a business is assigning the lease. Where large sums of cash being transferred are dependent on a landlord agreeing to the transfer of the lease, you can bet your socks many landlords are going to use this as an opportunity to leverage the outgoing tenant. It can get really messy.

If you've built your business well, and your staff is well trained, you are not just selling a cash stream, you're selling what people want the most. Time. Almost without exception, if you peel back the layers of what motivates people to work and achieve more financially, you'll eventually arrive at time as being at the core of their dreams. The Time to see their kids. Time to travel. Time to learn a new language. Time to just think.

A good Amazon business, well branded, well managed, and positioned for more growth, could be a very valuable asset to all kinds of buyers. So let's talk about those buyers, and then I'll give you some very specific advice about what you need to do in order to maximize your sale price.

The first kind of buyer, and possibly the one to pay more is a larger company selling similar products as you, but who perhaps doesn't understand Amazon as well as you. It is very often the case, with larger companies, that Amazon is just one of many distribution channels for their products and they therefore don't really understand the jungle like you do. After all, you have earned your livelihood from Amazon only, whereas they have all kinds of revenue streams to keep them alive.

A great example of the motivation behind this kind of buyer is in the Dollar Shave Club acquisition I referred to earlier in this book. Dollar Shave Club was purchased by consumer product behemoth, Unilever, for five times their projected revenue in the year of sale. This is an insane valuation for a private sale, so why did Unilever pay so much?

The answer is two-fold. First, Dollar Shave Club showed exceptional acuity regarding the leverage of social media and creating the kind of buzz that large companies only dream about. Their now-famous YouTube video has (at the time of me writing this book), been viewed more than 24,000,000 times. Who would have known that literally stating, "Our blades are f&^%$ing great!" would work so well?

While Unilever is a master of traditional advertising, the new world of social media and viral content is not their strong suit.

The other reason they paid so much, is because Dollar Shave Club had built a valuable brand connection with their audience. The fact they got to $150,000,000 in sales in just four years was impressive.

To a normal buyer, only looking at it from a cash flow point of view, Dollar Shave Club would have only been worth a multiple of its profits. To a company like Unilever, however, where they can leverage the intellectual property of the minds at Dollar Shave Club across other brand properties they own, the company is worth far more.

So if you become a successful monkey, peacock, or pea-monkey on Amazon, your first type of buyer might be a bigger player who wants not only your brand and cash flow, but your intellectual property as well so they can leverage what you know across the rest of their products.

Makes sense, right?

The second type of buyer is going to be a private buyer. These could include either a company or a private person, but in either scenario, they are most likely going to value your business on a multiple of its earnings (net profit before tax).

Important to these buyers are six key elements:

1. An upward sales trend
2. Diversified income source
3. Clean financials
4. Not key-person dependent
5. A logical reason for sale
6. Upside in the future

So let's begin with #1 - an upwards sales trend.

This one is quite obvious. It is always better to sell a business when the revenue history is tracking up and to the right and not down. This is where you, as an entrepreneur, need to plan well in advance, always pushing to make sure this year is better than the last.

The second thing buyers like to see is a diversified income source. As an Amazon seller, you can achieve this in two ways. First, you should have a *range* of products, rather than just one or two. Second, you should expand off Amazon, making sales on other marketplaces as well, or you should get the business ready for such expansion and hand it to them on a silver platter when they take over.

In the last couple of years, I've received written approval to sell on walmart.com as well as jet.com (which is owned by Walmart). I've also spoken to ChannelAdvisor.com who provide a platform enabling you to cross list your Amazon inventory into dozens of other market places around the world, including Tesco, Sears, eBay, shop.com, and many others.

These approvals, even if you haven't exercised them yet, add real value to an incoming buyer because they see specific op-portunities they can execute on immediately to add significant value to their new acquisition.

The third thing buyers look for is a clean set of books. This is critical, especially if the buyer is borrowing money to buy your business. Simply put, banks need to see a full set of accounts and a clean set of up-to-date tax returns before they'll lend money to anyone. If you don't have these at the ready, then you not only look unprofessional, you won't be able to sell your business to a buyer who is borrowing. This is really not ideal because buyers using someone else's money to buy your business will most likely pay more than a buyer using his own.

If you want to avail yourself of these premium buyers, you have to play by the bank's rules and get on top of your accounting early on.

When it comes to Amazon accounting, I use two pieces of software and a freelance bookkeeper. The software I use is:

- www.xero.com
- www.a2xaccounting.com

Xero is the accounting engine, and A2X connects Xero to my Amazon account. Once connected, A2X pulls in all of my sales, Amazon fees, and even my inventory. This last part, the inventory, is key. If you don't have accounting tools that can quantify your inventory levels and assign its value to your balance sheet, it can feel like you're going nowhere for a long time.

Remember the Marshmallow test? If you're smart and you follow Nike's lead, it's your *inventory levels* that will be growing for quite some time, not your bank balance. At the beginning of your inventory-based business (which Amazon is), the trick is to train your mind in a whole new way. Most small business people measure financial success by their bank balance, monthly paycheck, or end of year bonus. As an Amazon seller, while you're building, the metric you want to watch and celebrate is your growing inventory base. In simple terms, your inventory = more houses on the Monopoly board. In time, this equals cash flow that will keep coming long after you stop finding new houses to buy.

Make sense?

Now, seeing as we are talking about the idea of selling your business, this inventory build is also the cherry on top when you sell. No matter who buys your business, the valuation will always be done on some multiple of your net profit (before tax), or of your gross sales. There are many ways of arriving at a price for the actual *business*. The value of the inventory, however, is always assessed separately and purchased at cost on top.

Let's say your business is netting $300,000 profit, before tax, as an example, and you agree to a valuation of 3X profit. That's 3 x $300,000 = $900,000. You will then have to find out how much inventory you have and what it cost to manufacture, package, ship, and pay duties on, because the buyer will also need that inventory to carry on the business. For a business of that size, it is not unusual to have $100,000 worth of inventory sitting in Amazon's warehouses that you have slowly built up over time by not spending the profits.

When settlement day comes, you'll get the $900,000 for the business and then $100,000 for the inventory (or whatever the value is on the day of handover – again, why you need your real-time accounting tools in place). In total, you get a nice round check for $1,000,000.

I cannot emphasize enough how important it is that you set up your books with a professional from day one. If you don't, bad practices can, and almost always *do*, set in. We all know this to be true when it comes to tax time each year.

In an ideal world, you should be building this Amazon business in the same way as you might set up a long-term savings account or mutual fund. When you set these investments up, you are asked, "Would you like to automatically re-invest the interest and dividends?" Your advisor always tells you to tick "yes", right? It's the same at Amazon. Just re-invest your profits. The difference is your return is higher, comes much faster, and compounds at a staggering rate when compared to traditional savings plans and investments.

If you do take my advice here, and let the business grow for three to five years without pulling out cash for personal expenses, you could be sitting on a very nice portfolio of Amazon houses at the end. You can then cash out, or you could live off the income. What's important from an accounting point of view, is how relatively simple either cashing out or living off the income is.

In my business, I have only one income source to track: Amazon - with four payments a month. Two are from Amazon in the US, and two from Amazon in Europe. That's it. Just four incoming transactions per month.

Then, on the *outgoing* side, I only have two payees: my supplier in China and my freight forwarder.

Aside from those four incoming deposits, and those two outgoing payees, there's almost nothing else going in or out of the bank account. This makes your books super clean and your business very transparent (and attractive) to a buyer.

It's when you start randomly pulling money out of the business for personal expenses things start to get messy. Your book-keeper has to categorize each transaction and then, when it comes time to sell, you have to prove that the money you took, or the bill that you paid through the company, was actually a personal expense and not a bill that they will have to pay if they buy the business. If it's not absolutely clear and the buyer believes some of your personal expenses are actually business costs, it can be really expensive when it comes time to sell. Let me give you an example.

Let's say you have an expense in your accounts for $30,000 to attend the Canton Fair in China twice a year. In reality, visiting China might only cost $10,000 but you've been doing a side trip to Bali for two weeks and "putting it all through the busi-ness". In other words, you've hidden $20,000 of income by clas-sifying it as an expense. Not only is this a little dubious from a taxation perspective, it can be quite expensive and difficult to have to explain when it comes time to sell. Let me explain.

Let's say you have agreed to a valuation of 3X your profit plus the value of your inventory. In the example above, there's $20,000 of *income* hiding as an *expense* in your accounts. Had you properly allocated the $20,000 as *income* to yourself, you would have been able to charge $60,000 more for your busi-ness. Why? Because they are paying you 3X your profit, and now the $20,000 shows as profit to you, and not an expense to the business. Sure, you would have paid some tax on that $20,000 over the years as you took it as profit, but not $60,000!

Yes, you can explain to the buyer you hid $20,000 of income by marking it as an expense in your books, but this may make you look a bit sketchy and doesn't change the fact the buyer is probably borrowing money against your actual tax returns, not your notations around them.

Make sense?

You've probably heard the saying, "Begin with the end in mind." These days, I start every business as if I am going to sell it one day because it forces this kinds of discipline that is good for me. Remember how I said the following about selling a business at the start of this chapter?

"More than the money, who you become through the process is the real reward."

That's so true! If you can build and sell a clean and straight business, you have elevated yourself from relying on others for your income (a job), to knowing how to make your own income (business ownership), to knowing how to make businesses others earn their income from (business builder). More importantly, you have gone from being the tenant who pays the rent to the developer building the houses.

Most people have poor discipline because they have no clear end in mind for their life, their business, their health, or their relationships. They just go with the flow. As the saying goes,

"People who aim at nothing usually hit their target with amazing accuracy." Don't be one of those people!

Talent, without a clearly defined goal, quickly becomes a mess. Now I'm over 40 and doing business for more than 20 years, I've had many opportunities to observe the squandering of remarkable talent. It's heart breaking!

I've seen many of my own friends drink too much, party too hard, and generally mess up their lives, all by their 40th birthday. A lot of it was because they didn't create a clear and compelling vision for their life, one they could articulate clearly at a moments' notice. Because of this lack of clarity, they never really made decisions for themselves. Instead, they ended up *managing* what life gave them, rather than pushing back hard and saying, "No! *This* is what I want," and taking steps to make that happen.

Don't get me wrong, I understand as much as anyone that life isn't a personal development book and things rarely go as planned. That being said, I also know most of us could do a *lot* more with regards to planning our lives and being clear about what we want.

The way I see it, our lives are incredibly precious, but many of us treat ours with contempt and indifference. Here's an easy and fun way to start bringing some juice back to your everyday experience of life…

Next time someone asks how you're doing? Look them straight in the eye, light up a big smile, and say, "I'm amazing!"

I'm serious.

You will be amazed at the impact this has, not only on them but on you as well!

Nobody does this because they're all stuck in "I'm good" or "I'm OK" or "Not bad". WTF? "Not bad"? If God is listening, she'd have every right to be pretty pissed at you for rating her work so poorly!

The *truth* is you *are* amazing. Have you studied what it takes in order for you to see? Do you have any idea of the millions of miracles that have to occur simultaneously for you to be aware you're alive? Do you know how many people are starving right now while you leave half of your lunch in the trash?

We humans, especially in the West, have an enormous capacity to minimize the "amazing" in our lives, and maximize the tiniest bullshit problems leading to sub-standard evaluations of how we're doing.

So start by waking up and remembering this truth: You *are* amazing. You *are* lucky. You *are* blessed beyond measure. This is not only good for your mood, it's good for your business and it's the foundation of happiness. As I always like to say:

"Happiness is the unavoidable consequence of gratitude."

I've been telling people I'm amazing for years now. In fact, in the cafe near one of my homes, whenever I walk in they call me "Mr. Amazing" - without any cynicism. They love the fact that when I walk in they are all reminded to lift their game and re-member how good life is.

I could tell you story after story about the impact of my game, but one I will share was an encounter I had with an Uber driver who picked me up on Santa Monica Boulevard in Los Angeles. I was heading down to Hermosa Beach for a business meeting when the young driver asked me, "How are you going today, Adam?"

You guessed it, I was amazing.

Like everyone who asks, their curiosity kicks in and they ask, "Oh wow! That's an awesome response, why are you amazing? Did something cool happen?"

The discussion about what defines amazing begins.

I started by telling him my story about how I had suffered from debilitating panic attacks and anxiety after working myself too hard in my late thirties, and how I took time out to attend a Yoga and meditation retreat in Bali. That's where I met my happiness mentor, a guy who had survived cancer in his early twenties, and had dedicated his life since to helping stressed out people from all over the world reconnect with their passion and rediscover the amazing in life.

I then pointed out to this 20-something kid, driving Uber to support his acting dreams, how he was blessed beyond measure to have this opportunity.

"How lucky are you! Here you are, driving around Los Angeles in the sunshine, with Mr. Amazing in the back seat, being paid to meet cool people while you look at the ocean. Do you know how many people all over the world would kill for just one day in your life?"

The kid's wheels started turning. By the time I got out of the car, he was pumped. He didn't want me to leave!

As I left I said to him,

"Never forget that you are *amazing* and *blessed* beyond measure. Don't ever let people or social media trick you into thinking otherwise."

We both were beaming.

All of that came from simply saying two powerful words, "I'm amazing".

If you're ready to start setting a clear and compelling vision for your life and plan for your money, I have four great book recommendations for you on this stuff:

1. The Perfect Day Formula by Craig Ballantyne

2. The Magic Of Thinking Big by David Schwartz

3. The Richest Man In Babylon by George Clason

4. Think & Grow Rich by Napoleon Hill

All four of these books are life changing.

Ok, now back to the business stuff…

What else can you do to maximize the value of your business in the event of a sale?

Let's revisit the list of things I outlined earlier:

1. An upward sales trend
2. Diversified income source
3. Clean financials
4. Not key-person dependent
5. A logical reason for sale
6. Upside in the future

We are going to assume that #1 (an upwards sales trend) is in place. We've just spoken about #3 (clean financials) and we also covered the importance of training people well, so #4 is in place too.

So this leaves us with:

#2 - Diversified income source
#5 - A logical reason for sale
#6 - Upside in the future

Let's start with #5, a logical reason for the sale.

Naturally, people want to satisfy the nagging question: "If this business is so great, why are they selling it?"

Nobody, actually, wants to hear you desperately want to buy a nice house, take two years off in Tahiti, or buy a Lamborghini. They want to hear something that makes them feel like there's something in it for them, so you might want to craft an answer to appeal to *their* needs, not yours. I am not talking about lying here at all. I am just telling you it's smart to put yourself in their shoes and answer this question from that point of view..

I often find that the best answer is the simplest.

"I'm selling the business because I'm tired. I know the business can do better than it is now, I just don't have the energy anymore."

What do incoming buyers have that you probably don't? Energy! They are fresh, excited, and brimming with new ideas. You, on the other hand, have been grinding it out, compounding your profits, and reinvesting them back into the business. You built the beautiful home, now they get to live in it - for a price.

This answer is honest, it's simple, and it makes sense to buyers. It also sews the seed that there is more potential in this business, which in almost all cases, is true. So that's the approach I would take.

Now, let's talk about #2 (diversified income) and #6 (upside in the future).

As mentioned earlier in this chapter, selling on Amazon is amazing in so many ways, but it also carries some risk because your entire income stream is dependent on one relationship with one platform. Sure, it's a solid company, but nobody likes to be reliant on one source of income. Heck, that's like relying on a job. We all know how risky that is these days!

Just like your Amazon income becomes safer once it's coming from several Amazon properties (products), your *business* becomes safer when the money is arriving from different platforms.

If you're planning to sell, this is where you may want to consider launching into other marketplaces like eBay, Sears, walmart. com and jet.com. If that's too expensive, then at least go through the application processes and get approvals to sell in those marketplaces so the new buyer coming in can see a clear path to both diversifying their income and create substantial upside into the future.

Make sense?

What you want to be able to demonstrate is you're only just beginning in terms of how far your brand can go. You want to be able to show a clear path to them making a lot more money from your brand and increasing the value of their investment substantially. The clearer the path, the more value will be applied to your business.

This is not rocket science, but so few people think about this stuff by truly putting themselves in the shoes of the buyer and making plans to help them make more money *after* the sale occurs.

I *want* my buyers to make a ton more money than I did. I want them to succeed in a big way so I can look back and point to that company in five years' time and say, "I founded that company and look how successful it is now."

This then becomes part of your story to use to raise funds for future projects and do all kinds of other things.

This is not about win-lose. It's about showing your buyer how to win bigger, and if necessary, helping them to do it!

One of my mentors used to say to me, "Always leave enough on the table for the next person. That's the key to long term success you can be proud of."

To summarize, I believe that building and selling a business (in an ethical way), is not only financially intelligent, but one of the most rewarding projects you can undertake in your business life.

It takes courage, passion, creativity, discipline and patience - things that make you better in so many ways, both inside and outside of the business arena.

CHAPTER 11

★★★★★

AMAZON **SUPPORT**, ONLINE **COMMUNITIES** AND **MASTERMINDS**

According to a 2015 shareholder letter from Jeff Bezos (Amazon founder and CEO), there are now in excess of 2,000,000 Amazon sellers worldwide. This is a mind-boggling number of businesses, all vying for a piece of the pie. It also highlights just how high the demand is for goods on Amazon.

Not a week goes by where one of my students from somewhere in the world isn't posting their results on our private Facebook community, showing us that they just made $20,000 in a month, $50,000 in a month, or sometimes more! These are *new* sellers, arriving now, and they're doing great!

As a result of this sheer volume of sellers, information and support groups are to be found everywhere. The key is getting the *right* information and the *right* seller groups aligned with *your* values and business methodology.

Of course, there is no single correct way to do any of this. Be aware that just like the Amazon jungle, there are Monkeys, Peacocks, and Sloths selling courses, hosting webinars, and offering access to private mastermind groups. You must be vigilant in keeping your enthusiasm in check, and be careful you're not listening to someone who goes on and on about top line revenue numbers without discussing the underlying capital and time that's necessary to achieve those figures.

You also need to listen very carefully as to *how* they explain you should get there. Are they teaching Monkey tactics or Peacock tactics? Long or short term? How easy is it for others to do what they're advising? Is there substance or is it just hype?

At Reliable Education, we sell an online course following the basic themes outlined in this book, but it goes into much more detail and into many other nuanced areas of starting and scaling an Amazon business.

In addition to the course, you get access to our private Facebook community which is full of high-quality people all sharing a similar mindset about how to build a reliable income over time by compounding their profits and using them to grow a portfolio of Amazon houses and hotels.

In some cases, our students were already selling on Amazon when they found us. The reasons they signed up vary, but they often include:

- Having bought a course from a monkey, they started their business in microclimates full of monkeys, with more arriving every day. Their profits were always under attack and they didn't know why.
- They were successful on Amazon but missing a sense of community.
- They had come to realize the value of Peacock thinking and wanted to learn how to build a brand rather than just learning how to sell stuff at a margin.

I am always delighted when experienced sellers join us.

Without doubt, being part of a community is one of the most powerful things you can do to assist you in your success. It's where you'll go for fuel, support, and advice.

I usually post on the Reliable Education community a couple of times a week, usually videos from all over the world. This week I did some motivational videos from the top of Runyon Canyon in the Hollywood Hills. Last week I was in Singapore, and I shared a story of how I screwed up an order that ended up costing me a bunch of money (and how to avoid making the same mistake I made!)

Without question though, the best posts are from real students. It is remarkable watching someone post their introductory post, and then a few months later, seeing an update of their progress. Then, about six to nine months down the line, they post a screen shot of their income. It's so inspiring.

If you're interested in learning more about our program, go to www.reliable.education and enroll in the free video course that is advertised all over the website. You'll then receive information about how to join our paid program as well, if you're interested.

The other really cool thing about joining Reliable Education is that we proactively assist you to join a MasterMind of up to seven people, all of whom are doing the Reliable Income course. We give you a structure to run your meetings and provide a confidentiality agreement you can all sign so you feel safe sharing your ideas. These have proven to be really effective in keeping people on track and moving forward.

These MasterMinds occur both in-person and online, using video conferencing platforms like Google Hangouts and Zoom. To date, we have Masterminds in about a dozen countries and counting.

Aside from joining a community like ours for support, when you open your seller account with Amazon, you'll also be able to get help directly from them for technical questions. They have an extensive online database of support questions and answers, and they provide a free, instant callback service if you want to talk to someone. You simply login to your seller central account, go to the support area, and you'll find your way to the callback option. You put in your phone number, and within 10 seconds, your phone will ring with an Amazon support agent on the other end. It's remarkable.

The reason I added this chapter is because one thing about building an online business that *isn't* wonderful for most people is that it's a lonely road at times. Very often, you stay up late, trying to figure things out by yourself, and it can feel very lonely at times. It's easy to start second-guessing yourself.

Also, no matter what products you sell, there will be ups and downs in your journey. Sometimes you can inspire people in your support group because you're the one crushing it, while at other times, you'll be the one needing support. That's business and it's why many business people, even outside of Amazon, form MasterMind groups and professional networks.

My final word about getting help is this:

Never be afraid to invest in experts to help you.

Yes, I am not completely objective because I sell a course, but I can honestly say that education is rarely more expensive than ignorance. In my own businesses, my staff will often recite my line, "Never be afraid to pay for an expert, because real experts never cost you money."

It's true!

What costs you time and money in business is mistakes, and mistakes are often caused by lack of knowledge. That's why it's always smart to hire the smartest people you can find, who have done what you're trying to do.

Now, let's close out with something really special.

CHAPTER 12

★★★★★

MAKE IT **MATTER**

"Did you live? Did you love? Did you matter?"

— *Brendon Burchard*

Brendon Burchard is one of my favorite personal growth experts. If you haven't learned from him yet, go visit his website at www.brendon.com. The questions above were asked of me in a program I bought from Brendon, and they really get at the heart of what it means to live a fulfilling life.

While you might, right now, be focused on making a little extra money by starting an Amazon business, I'd like you to take a minute to ask yourself this question:

"Why do you want more money?"

It's a very simple question that I often ask people who attended my live seminars. Invariably, I get answers like this:

"I want to buy a bigger house"
"I want to buy a Ferrari"
"I want to work less so I can spend more time with my kids"
"I want to travel more"

No matter what the first answer is, I follow it up by asking:

"Why?"

Why do you want a bigger house?

Why do you want a Ferrari?

Why do you want to spend more time with your kids?

Why do you want to travel more?

The answers then come back like this:

"If I had a bigger house, my kids would have more room to play."

"If I had a Ferrari, I'd have a lot of fun and I think I'd get more girls."

"I want to spend more time with my kids because they're growing up so fast."

"If I travel more, my life would be more interesting."

If I keep peeling the onion of what's *really* driving their desire for these things, by asking *why* again and again and again, everybody arrives at the same point.

Everyone wants to be happier.

Here's the thing about happiness.

You can have it now, even before you have the thing you're saying will bring it to you.

If you live in the first world, and your basic needs such food and shelter is met, then happiness is something you make every day. It's not something that arrives after 'a thing' is acquired.

Let me share part of my own journey toward realizing this truth.

In 2016, all of my companies signed on to the Evolved Enterprise movement. Founded by my friend Yanik Silver, an internet-marketing pioneer turned force-for-good. This is a global community of entrepreneurs committed to *giving* as part of their business model. The simplicity and power of giving becomes immediately evident when you do it and the energy within your company changes.

By giving, you are forced to focus on people less fortunate than you are. This, in turn, triggers what I spoke about earlier - gratitude. Remember what I said about gratitude?

"Happiness is the unavoidable consequence of gratitude."

Rather than go on about the benefits of gratitude again, what I'd like to do is give you a practical way to embed gratitude into your business from day #1, even *before* it's profitable. No matter how much you decide to give, the effect of committing to something that *isn't* directly focused on your financial bottom line will be immediate and profound.

In my education company, we started very small. We began by pledging that we would do a micro-loan of $25 through kiva.org every time someone bought one of our courses. I have been a Kiva lender for years so this was an easy starting point.

Kiva is an awesome organization connecting lenders like me to people (mostly in third world countries) who need money to fund their education or business. They have people on the ground all over the world, organizing the borrowers and managing the repayment of the funds.

Over the years, I've done hundreds of loans, and my repayment rate has been almost 100%. What's really great about this program is you are empowering these people by *lending* the money (interest free), rather than just *giving* them money. They don't want hand outs either!

Because the money almost always comes back, the same loan of $25 can go on perpetually, reaching many more people over time.

Aside from the good this does externally, the impact this giving has had on our business has been profound. Our employees are profoundly inspired by what we are doing, and our customers love knowing that as they begin their journey of learning with us, in the hope they can improve *their* financial situation, they are also helping someone far less fortunate to improve their lot in life. It's a perfect fit.

To illustrate how deep this impact can be internally, we recently made 300 loans through Kiva, and one of our employees in South Africa asked if her kids could pick the loans. It had become a bit of a task to choose that many borrowers all at once, so we were more than happy to let her kids do it.

A few weeks later, she reported back that her children had read hundreds of borrower profiles, and picked what they believed were the 300 people that they could help the most. How great is that? Kids in South Africa spending their free time thinking about other people's situations that are considerably worse than theirs instead of sitting on Facebook all day, comparing themselves to the carefully manicured profiles of the world's privileged.

Taking it one step further, I also believe that giving actually makes money. I cannot really prove it, but I feel certain we have made more sales and had less fund requests because of our modest social activism. People just feel differently about who you are as a company, and they think more about how lucky they are when you remind them through your giving.

In the past, social responsibility was something you thought about once you were successful, whereas now, in the age of global connectivity and heightened awareness about almost everything, social responsibility is expected.

I truly believe that giving is kind *and* profitable.

As we've grown as a company, we have expanded our giving, and these days work with an organization curing people of blindness. I learned about this work while watching TV on a flight between Singapore and Los Angeles. The documentary showed these two blind sisters, both children, living in India. The documentary followed them and their parents from their poor village to one of the treatment centers where they could get free eye surgery to remove the cataracts that caused their blindness.

Incredibly, this surgery costs around $100 for the equipment, the doctors and all the rest, yet $100 is simply too much for these poor families. Imagine having two blind children when the cure is only $200?

In the documentary, these two beautiful girls got the surgery and their eyes bandaged so that they could rest. That night, they slept curled up in the arms of their parents who gently sang them to sleep with a lullaby. The next morning, they were led back to the clinic to have their bandages removed. As the bandages came off, light poured into their eyes without the hazy filter of a cataract to blind them. Smiles as bright as the morning sun lit their faces, as they saw their parents and the world, for the very first time.

If you can watch that and not cry, you are made of some pretty hard stuff. I wept like a baby! I also made a decision right there to make this part of our company's social program and I wanted to participate in it first hand.

Today, we sponsor entire villages of up to 2,000 people to get free eye examinations. Of this number, around 200 blind people have their vision completely restored, 300 people get glasses, and 10 people get glass eyes. We actually go into the villages with the doctors and support team, experiencing it first-hand. It is easily the one thing inspiring me the most these days.

What's so life changing about this work is that it's not just eyesight you're giving. You're actually breaking the poverty cycle. Many of these people are blind simply because they're poor. They can't afford the surgery. They can't afford the surgery because they're blind and cannot work. It's a totally breakable cycle! All they need is the money!

As my mentor Brendon asked, "Did you live? Did you love? Did you matter?"

Who knew that fulfilling these three questions was as simple as giving to someone else?

So to close this book, I encourage you to think deeply about not only what it is that you want from your life and business, but also who you'd like to inspire and help as well. I have learned, after many years of doing business, the one thing people struggle with most is motivation, your reason to get up and make it happen. You cannot train people to be motivated.

So work on your compelling vision, your reason for doing something extraordinary. In the same way, having children often inspires people to get their act together, you'll be amazed at what happens when you expand your inspiration to include others.

Thank you for reading my book and I wish you every success in building an incredible Amazon business!

CHAPTER 13

★★★★★

CONNECT WITH ADAM

RELIABLE EDUCATION

Reliable Education is focused on providing quality training on how to build a thriving eCommerce business, starting with the Amazon marketplace. That training is delivered through a combination of online lessons, private Facebook groups, live conferences, live and virtual mastermind groups and email support.

Reliable Education was founded on the idea that for most people, an Amazon or eCommerce business should be started as a side project that, through continuous reinvestment of profits over time, grows into a reliable income stream that can replace or supplement a full time job or other business income.

Learn more at www.reliable.education

ZON GURU

Zon Guru is a software company focused on making Amazon seller's lives easier. It does that by providing a suite of tools including:

- Sales Spy – an inventory tracking tool that reveals the daily sales of products sold on Amazon.

- Email Automator - an email tool that enables sellers to setup a sequence of emails that are delivered to Amazon customers through Amazon's platform.

- Dashboard – a tool that gives sellers greater insight into what their net profit is, which products are performing the best through advertising, and even a valuation widget that calculates the potential value of their Amazon business based on real sales data over whatever time period the user decides.

Adam developed ZonGuru to solve problems that he was facing as a seller.

Learn more at www.zonguru.com

SELLER PHOTO

Seller Photo is a full service product photography business that works for all kinds of eCommerce companies. The company specializes exclusively in product photography.

Hiring only the best product photographers, the company offers a broad range of services including everything from white background studio shots, to hand modelling and on-location shoots.

Learn more at www.sellerphoto.com

Made in the USA
Middletown, DE
07 September 2018